BUDDHA'S
BODYGUARD

"Jeff Eisenberg is one of the most refreshing voices in Buddhist teaching. His emphasis on the practical resonated with me since I first encountered his first book, *Fighting Buddha*, and in this latest volume he continues to teach us how to translate practice into workable action. Jeff empowers us to be our own bodyguards in a physical, mental, emotional, and spiritual sense, and for this offering I am grateful. Be prepared for some major internal shifts upon picking up this clever read!"

— JAMIE MARICH, Ph.D., trauma specialist, Gracie Jiu-Jitsu practitioner, and author of *Dancing Mindfulness* and *EMDR Therapy and Mindfulness for Trauma-Focused Care*

"Drawing from his experiential knowledge of being a Buddhist practitioner, professional bodyguard, and martial artist, Jeff Eisenberg delivers wisdom on personal protection of body, mind, and spirit."

— SHAWN ZAPPO, surf instructor, meditation teacher, and writer

"Another gem, or should I say 'Dharma Jewel' from Mr. Eisenberg! The Buddha's teachings from the world of protection and safety walk side by side in this wonderfully written manual. Practical and always entertaining. Even if you have never set foot inside a Buddhist temple, or have been a bodyguard, you will learn a helluvalot from this book! I highly recommend it."

— DAVID "SHINZEN" NELSON, Ph.D., author of *Black Belt Healing: A Martial Artist's Guide to Pain Management and Injury Recovery*

BUDDHA'S
BODYGUARD

How to Protect Your Inner V.I.P.

JEFF EISENBERG

 FINDHORN PRESS

Findhorn Press
One Park Street
Rochester, Vermont 05767
www.findhornpress.com

Disclaimer
The information in this book is given in good faith and is neither intended to diagnose
any physical or mental condition nor to serve as a substitute for informed medical
advice or care. Please contact your health professional for medical advice and treatment.
Neither author nor publisher can be held liable by any person for any loss or damage
whatsoever which may arise from the use of this book or any of the information therein.

A CIP record for this title is available from the Library of Congress

ISBN 978-1-84409-740-1 (print)
ISBN 978-1-84409-758-6 (e-book)

Printed and bound in the United States by Versa Press, Inc.

10 9 8 7 6 5 4 3 2 1

Edited by Nicky Leach
Text design and layout by Damian Keenan
Illustrations: www.depositphotos.com
This book was typeset in Adobe Garamond Pro and Museo Sans with ITC Blair used as
a display typeface.

To send correspondence to the author of this book, mail a first-class letter to the
author c/o Inner Traditions • Bear & Company, One Park Street, Rochester, VT 05767,
and we will forward the communication, or contact the author directly at
www.fightingbuddhadojo.com

CONTENTS

FOREWORD

Jeff Eisenberg occupies a small niche in the Buddhist world. Actually, he *created* that niche, which is bad ass, and I'm very much hoping to see it expand. With 46 years of martial arts training and 33 years of Buddhist practice under his various black belts, Jeff's approach is startlingly unique. He recognizes the unfortunate necessity of violence in certain situations and is well versed in protecting himself and others. Buddhism is often seen as a completely pacifistic religion, concerned only with cultivating peace and compassion. And yet, it's Jeff's deep understanding of Buddhism and long-time meditation practice that inform his martial arts skills and allow him to respond to violence with violence in the least harmful way possible.

After years of training civilians, cops, and the military in self-defense, as well as providing private and personal security, Jeff has decided to transfer those talents to the realm of psycho-spiritual struggles. His specific skillset, so often used to provide protection for high-level executives and celebrities, is now being offered to those of us who fight our battles on the meditation cushion. Our inner peace, our sense of enlightenment and freedom, our internal Buddha: this is what Jeff is teaching us to safeguard.

He doesn't pull his punches, either. This isn't exactly a book for the casual practitioner, the New Age Dabbler, or the touchy-feely part-timers looking for less stress and better sex. This is for meditators ready to do the work, to clench their jaws, face their adversaries, and come out on top.

There are plenty of Buddhist authors out there willing to tell you this practice is tough but none of them can draw the parallels Jeff does. By comparing spiritual techniques to tactics used in the protection industry, he makes what is normally a mental endeavor visceral and sweaty. You're not going to feel clean and safe reading this; you're going to feel like you've been training to choke the shit out of all the personal demons you've created that stand between you and happiness.

Jeff mentions the martial arts saying, "Many will step on the mat but few will stay." I've done martial arts and I know this is true because I'm one of the many who quit. I thought I wanted to learn how to defend myself. I was attracted to the honor and discipline and tradition of martial arts. Turns out, they're not about that at all, at least if you want to actually be prepared for violence. They're about fighting and fighting is hard and scary and I was not cut out for it at all. The first time I got punched in the face, I had to take a few minutes to myself and put some serious thought into what I was doing. Once I got over it, somebody pounced on my back like a gorilla, wrapped their arms around my neck, and, near as I could tell, attempted to crush all the breathing life from my body. I tapped out immediately, which is the only aspect of fighting I naturally excelled at. Two days later, when I got my voice back, I said, "That's enough for me, thanks." I joined the long and ignominious parade of people who walked out the door but never walked back in.

The same is true in spiritual practice. Millions of people are interested in being happier, kinder, and more fully awake in this world. They see the Dalai Lama fumbling blissfully about, speaking in adorably broken English, and urging them to just be *nice* to each other and they think, "I want what that guy has." They join a local meditation group and, after a couple weeks or months, they quit because they aren't happier or kinder yet. What's more, meditation ended up being *hard*, even though it *looks* peaceful as hell.

I lead a weekly meditation group and I coach private mindfulness students. I've seen plenty of people show up excited to get going, only to fade away after a few short sessions. They wouldn't blink an eye if a fitness trainer told them it takes time and effort to get into better physical shape. Nor would they imagine they'd be sexy and ripped after two weeks at the gym. Yet they sort of unconsciously expect that from meditation practice. When it becomes apparent that it takes dedication and pain to change a lifetime of habits, traits, and slipshod morality, they respond like me after I got punched and strangled.

Even though Jeff is clear that protecting and nurturing your inner Buddha is strenuous, exhausting, and often boring, he doesn't make it seem impossible. He has a knack for making the reader feel like this is something they can do, despite the degree of difficulty. Additionally, he writes in easy-to-understand terms, many taken from the tactical world of security and protection. Don't let his casual tone and the absence of difficult Sanskrit words fool you; this is straight up dharma. It's obvious that Jeff has a deep understanding of traditional Buddhist theory, thought, and practice but, rather than presenting it in the same tired, academic way we've seen a thousand times, he comes across as a guy talking to you at the dojo after he's just beaten you up a little. He wants you to improve and it's readily apparent he knows his stuff forward and backward but he's not just throwing info at you, overwhelming you with needless jargon. Instead, he's illustrating his points with personal stories and showing you exactly how to get better, while never letting you think it's going to be an easy road. He's done the work and he can help you do it, too.

Jeff is an important voice in American Buddhism, which is all too often weak and ineffective. It takes toughness to walk this path, and a willingness to meet inner violence with love and acceptance, which is much harder than responding with brutality. But it also takes knowledge and experience, and the wisdom to know exactly when to apply force, and how much. Jeff is tough. He's also kind and loving. He's got the knowledge, the experience, and the wisdom. I'm thrilled he's taught me to kick some spiritual ass and I hope you get out there on the mat, too.

Brent R. Oliver

award-eligible writer, mindfulness coach,
Buddhist troublemaker, contemplative cross trainer
brentroliver.com *and* thetattooedbuddha.com

INTRODUCTION

I have taught thousands of students personal protection theory and techniques over the years, and I have always started the instruction with the same message:

> It is vital to realize that a physical altercation is the last thing that happens in a chain of events. And while we must never blame the victim, our safety is our responsibility.
>
> Many situations can be avoided or their severity greatly lessened, if we pay attention during the chain of events that leads up to the situation and respond appropriately.

Throughout my career as an investigator, bodyguard, tactics trainer, and martial arts instructor, I have heard numerous stories told by victims that range from the typical drunk jerk being a pain in the ass to horrific tales of violence, sexual assault, and hostage situations. More often than not, when the story was examined closely, it revealed that there were times in the chain of events when the victim's actions, or lack thereof, played a part in aiding the assailant.

Again, I am in no way blaming the victim! What I am saying is that we all have the chance to train ourselves to be more proactive in our own safety and avoid becoming a victim. And if we are victimized, our training will result in appropriate actions that will aid in our ability to survive with much less injury and trauma.

But this is *not* a book about personal protection, per se; it is a book that will take personal protection theory and specific tactics utilized by bodyguards and apply it *to* Buddhist practice, as it lays out strategies you can implement to protect your inner Buddha from attack.

Yeah, I'm a Buddhist. I was hoping that people would get that from the cool title I came up with, but if you didn't, now you know.

So, if you are a martial artist who bought this book to learn some badass martial arts techniques and have no interest in Buddhism, I'm sorry to disappoint you. But hang in there, as I think that you will find Buddhist teachings useful, regarding the mindset and strategies that go into a personal protection situation. Who knows? A little Buddhism might not hurt ya, either.

(By the way, if you're interested in more of a martial arts slant, I have another book with another cool title, *Fighting Buddha* (Findhorn Press, 2016) that you should check out. And if you want to train, you can contact me through www.fightingbuddhadojo.com. (I know, some serious self-promotion, but the books ain't paying all the bills!)

Conversely, if you are already a Buddhist but have no interest in the martial arts, I think you'll find it very useful to learn how the strategy a bodyguard uses to protect a client can be applied to your Buddhist practice. In fact, I am hoping that you have already recognized some Buddhist buzz phrases ("chain of events" and "pay attention") that are reminiscent of "the twelve links of dependent origination" and "mindfulness," and that I've piqued your interest enough to continue reading—and you're not on your way back to the bookstore to demand a full refund.

So, if you are still with me, let's take a look at just what a bodyguard is … and is not.

1

BIGGER IS *NOT* BETTER

In the movie *The Bodyguard*, an ongoing joke throughout the movie is that whenever someone meets Kevin Costner (who plays the bodyguard in the movie, in case you haven't seen it), they give him the once-over and say, with a mix of surprise and disappointment, "I thought you'd be bigger."

When most people think of a bodyguard, they picture a huge, hulking, juiced-up, musclehead, towering over the client they are protecting, ready to tear someone limb from limb. But nothing could be farther from the truth. Most of the time, this type of bodyguard is there merely for appearances' sake. He's usually a childhood friend of the celebrity who was nice enough to give him a job. More often than not, rather than being a legitimate bodyguard, he ends up being more of a personal assistant, or worse, an errand boy who is being exploited by his "friend" to do menial tasks.

Ironically, not only does this type of bodyguard have *zero* protection skills, and cannot tear anyone limb from limb, but aside from being willing to run errands, their sole qualification is simply being *big*! I know it sounds ridiculous, but that's pretty much how it is. The VIP trusts their protection to an untrained Neanderthal who has no clue how to properly respond to a threat situation.

This is not just conjecture; I witnessed this firsthand when I was part of a team hired to train a major NBA star's new bodyguard. This trainee was exactly as I described earlier: merely a childhood friend with a large body and no experience whatsoever. He not only was completely unqualified for the job but, worse, could not have cared less about getting trained to do the job. He resisted us every step of the way by doing as little as he possibly could during the training. Not that he could have achieved much in the short time we were hired to work with him, but kudos to the NBA star for at least offering him some training.

It seems ridiculous, but doesn't that description also eerily fit how we face our lives much of the time? Don't we often entrust the safety of our inner Buddha to that untrained, hulking beast that has followed us around since childhood? More often than not, our unwholesome, unskilled, conditioned self habitually responds inappropriately by tearing *our* lives limb from limb. I know my beast is always around, and I'd guess that your beast is, too!

But we can do something to calm that beast and keep our inner Buddha safe from such incompetency and unprofessionalism! There is another type of bodyguard—someone who has spent years in intensive training, perfecting all aspects of threat prevention and crisis response; someone who, rather than rushing haphazardly into a threat scenario like our friend, the Neanderthal, is a professional with both a *pro*active and *re*active plan of expertly honed tactics; someone who can calmly and efficiently act and respond with appropriate countermeasures.

Like this type of bodyguard, we can utilize our Buddhist training to develop well-honed, skillful, and appropriate actions in response to the threats we face in our daily lives. We can train to avoid being abducted by greed, hate, and delusion. We can learn how to break free from being held hostage by our habitual pursuing and avoiding of things. We can practice how to take appropriate cover from the shrapnel of our explosive reactions. And we can train to safely evacuate from behind the enemy lines of attachment, pity, envy, and indifference. So does this mean that much of Buddhist practice is a knock-down, drag-out fight? The truth of the matter is that much of the time it is. I guess that's not what a newbie to Buddhism wants to hear, and I know the New Age crystal gazers just got their chakras in a bunch reading this tidbit of information, but it's true! Much of the time, Buddhist practice is a tedious, painful, frustrating process. Hell, if it wasn't, everyone would be an enlightened, blissful Buddha!

Of course the work is hard; that's why they call it work! But the harder the work, the greater the reward! So the fight is totally worth it, in order to liberate oneself from the oppressive grip of Mara's tyranny—Mara is a devil-like character found in Buddhist literature who acts as a metaphor for the hindrances we face in practice; much more on this later. It is the ultimate victory, and while available to all, only attained by the brave few who choose to go to battle for it.

An old Zen story puts it like this, "Many know of this, but few can speak of it." This story points to the fact that in spite of so many understanding the great reward that results from putting in the hard work required in Buddhist practice, few ever will or have the experience of those results.

An old martial arts adage says, "Many will step on the mat, but few will stay." That is, after the novelty of starting training wears off, most people quit, as that is when the hard work really starts. Beginners get their first important insight: that gaining proficiency takes long-term commitment to pursuing an arduous path, one that will push their resolve to the limit and demand nothing less than blood, sweat, and tears.

Another old martial arts adage, however, seems to contradict this: "Step on the mat once, train forever." This may seem like a contradictory statement, but what it means is that once you start training you will never stop, and even if you only train a single time, you will have to live with the fact that you quit for the rest of your life, as the lesson that comes from quitting is actually much harder than sticking with it. To be constantly reminded of one's failure, coupled with the knowledge of not facing that failure and remedying it, results in much greater pain and anguish than anything one ever experiences in persevering on the mat.

It is no different in Buddhist practice. In fact, as I will explain in this book, the First Noble Tactical Truth in the strategy for liberation I lay out is to acknowledge that we do have a fight on our hands. Our mission, should we choose to accept it, is to combat the threat of Mara; to intercept and terminate the attacks of greed, hate, and delusion; and extract ourselves from being taken hostage by our harmful conditioning and reactivity.

Like the old martial arts adages I mentioned earlier, the Buddhist practitioner's greatest lesson comes in realizing that surrender is not an option, and to persevere in fighting the good fight is the greatest victory of all. Like the martial artist who quits, the Buddhist practitioner who surrenders and abandons practice has an even more difficult path to walk, because rather than their practice benefitting them by helping to heal their past issues, they must now live with the ways in which quitting compounds those issues, which in turn increases their existing suffering.

I'm often asked, "How long does it take for the average person to achieve a black belt?" My response is always, "The average person will *never* achieve a black belt!" And the average person will *never* achieve the awakening and liberation that Buddhism has to offer either, as it takes nothing less than practicing with every fiber of one's being and the willingness to sacrifice everything!

Several old Buddhist legends point to the depth of dedication needed:

When the Indian monk Bodhidharma arrived in China, he retreated to a cave and sat staring at the cave's wall in meditation. In the seventh year of his sitting he fell asleep, and when he awoke he was so angry with himself for doing so that he cut his eyelids off so it would never happen again. He then sat with a fierce determination for another two years, until after a total of nine years he finally began teaching.

Years later, a student who wanted to study with Bodhidharma was held to the same level of dedication: Huike sat in vigil outside the Shaolin monastery, waiting for Bodhidharma to accept him as a student. He sat for weeks, through the horrendous conditions of a frigid winter, and still he was refused. It was only after he cut off his own arm that he was able to prove his worth as a student and was accepted into the monastery by Bodhidharma.

Of course, these are just metaphors. But the point they make is that we need to have an unshakable resolve and be willing to go to unimaginable lengths in our practice, if we wish to protect ourselves from suffering.

So if you accept this mission, please turn the page to begin being briefed on Operation Bodyguarding the Buddha. (Don't worry this book won't self-destruct if you choose not to!)

2

The Notorious VIP

When we think of a VIP who needs protecting, most people, even Buddhist practitioners, picture a head of state, a prominent politician, a movie or TV star, or an extremely wealthy person, rather than the most notorious VIP of all: the Buddha!

Buddhist teachings speak of us being enlightened already, and that the reason we practice is to discover this, to reveal this innate quality already within us. So whether you wish to call it your inner Buddha, your true nature, or even enlightenment itself, what we are protecting is no less important than the Buddha himself!

I am acutely aware that many practitioners, even knowing that it's all a play on words, will find my idea of the Buddha or their Buddha nature needing protection, and my use of the concept of "being his bodyguard" as a metaphor for practice, contradictory to their idea of the Buddha and the actualizing of their own Buddhist practice. This is because most practitioners think of the Buddha as *their* protector. They imagine him as a superhero, standing stoically between themselves and the forces of an evil supervillain, rather than him being a vulnerable VIP who needs the protection of a security detail under their own direction. And while I must admit this was exactly my idealistic vision of the Buddha and his teachings early on in my practice, what I discovered was that the Buddha's teachings were actually directives exactly opposite of this understanding.

But before I discuss this, let me give those of you who don't know it a quick briefing on how the man known as Siddhartha Gautama rose to prominence as the notorious VIP known today simply as the Buddha. For those readers who do know the story (and are about to read it for the umpteenth time), bear with me, as hopefully by presenting it free from its metaphysical trappings, and against the backdrop of a different context, I will be able to deepen its meaning for you.

Born into the Shakya clan in India in the fifth century BCE, Sid was the son of the clan's chief and lived a life of luxury. Raised to be a king, his father kept him cloistered, shielding him from the sufferings of the world and of religious teachings. Although he was provided with everything he could ever want or need, Siddhartha felt unfulfilled.

At age 29, this lack of fulfillment prompted Siddhartha to venture out of his cloistered setting. Upon doing so, he saw a sick person, an old person, and a decaying corpse—all experiences he had never had before, as he had been purposely shielded from them.

Being hit with this reality so shocked Siddhartha, he fell into a deep depression and, renouncing his regal destiny, set out as a wandering ascetic, determined to discover how to overcome the horrors of old age, sickness, and death. He spent years studying different disciplines with different masters, and while he achieved great levels of insight and ability in each, none were able to satisfy his quest.

In response to what he deemed the failure of what he called "indulgent" practices, he and other ascetics took to practicing self-mortification, severe deprivation of the body. After having almost starved himself to death, he collapsed and was found by a young girl who offered him some food. Having found that neither the path of extreme indulgence nor the path of extreme mortification was correct, Siddhartha realized that the middle way between extremes was the answer, and he accepted just enough food to satisfy the nourishment he needed.

Siddhartha's fundamental insight from this experience, which became the foundation of his middle-way discovery, was that in disciplining his mind he had freed himself from the desire, hatred, and ignorance that had fueled his suffering. As I mentioned earlier, the traditional teaching story depicting this experience of the constant threat of the demon Mara serves as a metaphor for Siddhartha combating his conditioned mind.

So Siddhartha's enlightenment experience—his transformation into the Buddha, or the Awakened One, and rise to stardom as the notorious VIP—came from seeing clearly that rather than any practice making him invulnerable, practice brought his vulnerabilities to light. He not only realized that his vulnerabilities needed protection but that their need for protection never diminished. He saw that it was his responsibility to protect himself. Which is why I conclude that the teachings are exactly opposite of an understanding of the superhero Buddha protecting *us*.

In the traditional version of the Buddha's life story, this is demonstrated by the fact that even after becoming enlightened and right up until his death, the Buddha was constantly defending himself from the threat of Mara. In modern practice, we see this point illustrated over and over again, as our harmful conditioning and habitual reactivity is so deeply embedded within our minds that it is continually challenging us. And while we are able to weaken it, what truly changes, is our relationship with it and our reaction in response to it.

What made the Buddha's insight so radical was that it was completely contrary to the common beliefs of the day, which involved dogmatic worship of deities and required practitioners to place all their hopes in gaining enough merit from practice that a spiritual superhero would come to their rescue and protect their soul from the forces of evil.

The Buddha's wakeup call was his realization that this protection humans yearned for, and desperately needed, was not to be found in a belief that involved a superman swooping in and saving the day, or signaling him with a type of ancient bat signal; rather, it was to be found in a grounded, reality-based understanding of the nature of the human condition and its experience, and the pragmatic action that one needs to take to save one's mind.

So in keeping with the bodyguard metaphor, in the chapters that follow, I will brief you on the Buddha's initial "threat assessment" and the first pragmatic directives that came from that assessment, which are the foundation strategies for my mission in writing this book. They are The Four Noble Tactical Truths, which details why suffering exists, how it begins, and how it ends, and The Eightfold Tactical Plan, which details the actions we must take to end it. I'll brief you on implementing these directives to keep your inner spiritual warrior safe from harm.

3

The First Noble Tactical Truth
"Suffering Exists"

Threats Exist

Security starts with the understanding that threats exist, that there will always be a threat we must face, and that we must always be prepared to face it. A naïve bodyguard thinks that with a perfect proactive plan they will be able to secure their client from all threats, whereas, an experienced bodyguard knows that it is impossible to secure the client completely, so they are always prepared with a reactive plan of securing and evacuating the client during a threat.

An inexperienced bodyguard's refusal to acknowledge the constant existence of a threat, and the civilian's belief that, when it comes to self-defense, "it will never happen to them," are exactly the beliefs that make them vulnerable. Likewise, the Buddhist practitioner's inability to comprehend the ongoing threat of suffering is the root of their suffering, as lacking that understanding they cannot formulate an appropriate preventive measure or respond when threats arise.

The First Noble Truth of Buddhism states that suffering exists, that there is a constant dissatisfaction that is inherent to life that makes the threat of suffering always present, and that it is our refusal to accept this reality that ultimately turns our pain into suffering.

Most people who seek out Buddhism think that practice will enable them to eliminate their pain and provide them with a state of permanent happiness. But the reality is that all that Buddhist practice will do is help

22

us develop the skills to cope with this constant dissatisfaction and not turn our pain into suffering.

The teachings speak of three truths that mark the existence of suffering, and that understanding them is essential to our ability to thwart suffering.

The first truth of the existence of suffering teaches that due to our body and mind, we will always be experiencing pain and that it is not the pain itself that causes us to suffer but our aversion to experiencing the pain. This aversion actually causes us to suffer over being in pain rather than from the pain itself. The result of this is that we compound our problems by never actually dealing with the issue that caused the pain in the first place.

To remedy this, the teachings direct us to realize that it is up to us to repeatedly practice how to engage our pain and simply be with it without adding anything to it, such as self-pity, judgment, anger, or resentment. By doing this, we are able to see that there is no magic teaching that instantaneously does this for us, or any wondrous level of attainment in our ability to do so, but rather, the more we practice doing it, the more skillful we will become at doing it. Much like a martial artist training physical actions of technique into their muscle memory, our ability to cope with and manage pain actually begins as a physical practice.

When we first encounter Buddhism, the first thing that most of us are introduced to is meditation. As we learn to sit in the meditation posture, the practice of being still and grounding ourselves in our physical experience (the first foundation of mindfulness, but more on that later) teaches us to experience our pain without being swept away by an inner dialogue about it—that rather than being a helpful coping mechanism, the dialogue we add creates the aversion that makes us suffer.

We learn that by engaging the painful experience, and observing it and investigating it, there is a constant ebb and flow of the temporary conditions at its foundation; we learn that eventually these conditions will change and the experience that is dependent on them will change as well, and due to this, there is no need served to be identified with them. As my teacher, Noah Levine, often says, "Pain is a given, but suffering is optional."

The second truth of the existence of suffering teaches that our suffering is due to our inability to accept change: we want things to be exactly the way we want them to be. And while it is our lack of flexibility in being able to accept that they are not that causes us pain, it is our continued effort to try and make them conform to the way we want them to be (most of the time in spite of it not even being possible) that turns that pain into suffering.

And then to make matters worse, on the rare occasion that things actually are the way we want them to be, we are so worried about them ending, we suffer and never end up enjoying them in the first place! What we ultimately learn is that if we face things as they are, rather than trying to make them the way we want them to be, we will not suffer.

The third truth of the existence of suffering teaches what Buddhism calls "conditionality." Conditionality is the phenomenon of an experience being dependent on a particular set of conditions coming together. In this context, it is referring to the experience we have from this process that results in what we perceive as the "self."

The teaching identifies these five conditions as:

1. Form
2. Feeling
3. Perception
4. Discrimination
5. Awareness

The teaching then goes on to define each condition and explains how the process of them interdepending (being inextricably linked) creates our experience.

As noted above, the teaching of this process begins with *form*. Form is defined as the sense organs, which are identified as the eyes, ears, nose, tongue, body, and mind. Form also includes the material objects the sense organs perceive, namely, things that are seen, heard, smelled, tasted, touched, and thought about.

It is from this contact with sense-object sensations that we experience *feeling* and identify the feeling experience as either pleasant or unpleasant.

As a result of the contact form makes via the sense organs, and the feeling that then rises from that contact, we develop *perception*. Perception is defined as our recognition of the sense object being perceived.

Our perception of the sense object then causes a mental formation, which is the basis of our *discrimination*. Discrimination is defined as the choosing of our actions based upon our recognition of the object of our perception.

This recognition then becomes *awareness*, which is the last condition. Awareness is defined as knowledge of the totality of what we are experiencing. But contrary to what we usually think, awareness is not a larger, independent function that monitors all the other conditions but an equal part of this process, just as dependent on the other conditions as they are on it. And while the process appears to have a linear trajectory, the traditional teaching describes the result of the coming together of these conditions as a singular experience: a *pile* or *heap*.

This truth of the existence of suffering, as it pertains to conditionality, is that we mistakenly believe these conditions to be solid, fixed, and permanent, rather than understanding them as a fluid process.

Understanding this is the starting point for our understanding of the workings of what is known as *dependent origination*, where we begin to experience how interdependence causes an interaction of the conditions we come to call "self," and how our identification with and attachment to the conditions causes us to suffer.

The teaching then goes deeper, explaining how our suffering is rooted in how we misunderstand the result of that experience and believe that we are something fixed and permanent, rather than understanding that because the conditions themselves are fluid and don't inherently exist, the experience of self that is dependent on them doesn't inherently exist, either.

It's at this point that people get a bit freaked out and mistakenly twist this teaching into "I don't exist." But the teaching does not tell us that we don't exist; rather, it tells us that we exist in a different way from how we think we do.

The problem we have with understanding the self is that our confusion is rooted in our having a wrong view of *emptiness*, in general, and of the empty aspect of the conditions themselves, in particular. This wrong view then deludes our perception of the resulting experience that is dependent upon them.

We don't understand that to say that something is "empty" is not the same as saying that it does not exist; it is merely recognizing that it only exists temporarily due to temporary conditions, and that it will eventually cease to exist when those conditions change. I'm sorry to tell you, but the truth is that *nothing* has a fixed, permanent, inherent existence, and this includes you and me.

But what we also misunderstand is that while the teaching says that a permanent self does not exist, this does not mean that we do not have a *personal* experience that is exclusively our own. It doesn't tell us to not pick or choose or to not have preferences or judgments; rather, it says that we should not be *attached* to our picking or choosing, preferences or judgments.

By being rigid about our judgments and choices, we think we are keeping ourselves whole and staying true to what defines us, that to relinquish any aspect of how we define ourselves would makes us less ourselves, when, in fact, what this does is restrict and limit us. It is only when we can let go of our narrow definition of self, and our need to stay true to how we've rigidly defined ourselves, that we discover our true self. This creates an expansive experience that opens us up and introduces us to new likes and preferences we had never let ourselves experience, or even knew we had.

If you're a bit confused and freaked out right now, don't worry, as it's an absolutely normal part of practice we all must go through. But do not think that your confusion or your freaking out is a result of your inability to tune in to some hippy-dippy New Age stuff, as it's actually a result of the exact opposite. Meaning that, rather than emptiness being some supernatural, trippy experience, it actually is the most concrete, down-to-earth, reality-based understanding of our existence we can have! So rather than trying to blow your mind sky high, Buddhism is actually trying to bring it back down to earth and ground it in reality.

Before we go deeper into this teaching, let's first take a look at an example of how things we think exist really do not.

Since I'm a martial artist, I'll start off with my favorite example: a fist. I know that I touched upon this example in my first book, *Fighting Buddha*, but bear with me, as this version is much more extensive. (Oh, and thank you for reading *Fighting Buddha*, and I hope, buying it!)

When I say the word "fist," it creates an instant mental image, and you know exactly what I mean. But if we take a good look at a fist, we see that it is the result of the brain sending an impulse down the arm and to the hand. The hand is made up of five fingers, which, when they receive the impulse, bend together toward the palm and close, making a fist. But when a new impulse from the brain shoots down through the arm and reaches the hand and fingers, telling them to open, the fist no longer exists, as the temporary conditions needed for its existence have changed.

Now, imagine if the impulse that was sent by the brain down the arm into the hand and fingers was to close three fingers and hold up two. Well, then you'd say a peace sign existed, but you'd be wrong about that, too. Or what if the impulse that shot down the arm into the hand and fingers was to close four fingers and just hold up the one middle finger? Well, that "fuck you" finger doesn't really exist, either.

Or does it? Of course it does. We all have had that angry response within us when someone flips us off! But we are not really reacting to a finger being held up, but rather the concept that we associate with it. So the finger itself is empty of any real fuck-you-ness. Fuck-you-ness only exists when the brain shoots the impulse down the arm to the hand and fingers to close four fingers and hold one up, and you see it and add a concept to it.

Ironically it turns out there is a long history of Zen masters teaching by giving people the finger!

> Gutei raised his finger whenever he was asked a question about Zen. A boy attendant began to imitate him in this way. When anyone asked the boy what his master had preached about, the boy would raise his finger. Gutei heard about the boy's mischief. He seized him and cut off his finger. The boy cried and ran away. Gutei called and stopped him. When the boy turned his head to Gutei, Gutei raised his own finger. In that instant the boy was enlightened.

Appealing to my penchant for irreverence and rebellion, as well as my love of martial arts fighting, here is one of my favorites:

Provided he makes and wins an argument about Buddhism with those who live there, any wandering monk can remain in a Zen temple. If he is defeated, he has to move on.

In a temple in the northern part of Japan, two brother monks were dwelling together. The elder one was learned, but the younger one was stupid and had but one eye.

A wandering monk came and asked for lodging, properly challenging them to a debate about the sublime teaching. The elder brother, tired that day from much studying, told the younger one to take his place. "Go and request the dialogue in silence," he cautioned. So the young monk and the stranger went to the shrine and sat down.

Shortly afterwards, the traveler rose and went in to the elder brother and said, "Your young brother is a wonderful fellow. He defeated me."

"Relate the dialogue to me," said the elder one.

"Well," explained the traveler, "first, I held up one finger, representing Buddha, the enlightened one. So he held up two fingers, signifying Buddha and his teaching. I held up three fingers, representing Buddha, his teaching, and his followers living the harmonious life. Then he shook his clenched fist in my face, indicating that all three come from one realization. Thus he won and so I have no right to remain here."

With this, the traveler left.

"Where is that guy?" asked the younger one, running into his elder brother's room.

"I understand you won the debate," the older brother responded.

"I won nothing," yelled the younger brother. "I am going to beat him up."

"Tell me the subject of the debate," asked the elder one.

"Why, the minute he saw me, he held up one finger, insulting me by insinuating that I have only one eye. Since he was a stranger, I thought I would be polite to him, so I held up two fingers, congratulating him that he has two eyes. Then the impolite wretch held up three fingers, suggesting that between us we only have three eyes. So I got mad and got ready to punch him, but he ran out and that ended it!"

A true understanding of emptiness can only come from experiencing it, although I don't suggest having your finger cut off or being punched in the face by a nonexistent fist to do so!

On second thought, getting punched in the face might be an excellent way to experience the emptiness of conditionality, as at least it's a real experience! Many people want to make conditionality and emptiness a far-out, lofty, metaphysical experience, but what's truly important about understanding conditionality is the role it plays in the context of a realistic, skillful application of the Buddha's teachings.

A Zen koan addresses this:

The master said to his student, "If you understand emptiness, grab it and show it to me!"

The student instantly responded by thrusting his arm out and grabbing the air with his hand.

"You understand nothing!" the mastered yelled, as the student held out his clenched fist to show the master the emptiness that he had grabbed.

Dejected and confused, as he had thought that he had the correct answer, the student pleaded, "Please master, show me emptiness!"

The master quickly reached out and grabbed the student's nose and twisted it hard until the student screamed with understanding.

The student's mistake was that he was stuck in understanding emptiness as a void, as nonexistence, or "nothingness." The Heart Sutra teaches us to not make this mistake by saying:

Form is no other than emptiness, emptiness no other than form.

The great Vietnamese Zen master Thich Nhat Hanh poetically teaches this by using a piece of paper as an example. He eloquently speaks about how a piece of paper both exists and does not exist by addressing how he sees both the piece of paper, as well as the conditions of its existence. These include the dirt, sunshine, water, and air that are needed by the tree to grow, as well as, the person who cuts down that tree, the person and elements needed to create the tool used by the person who cut down the tree with it, and all the conditions involved with turning that tree into sheets of paper.

It's not simply imaginative conjecture; Thich Nhat Hanh speaks directly from deeply experiencing both the piece of paper and the conditions that it's dependent on. Imagine if we could live our lives so deeply! We'd be constantly filled with gratitude for everything.

So getting back to how this teaching applies to our understanding of the "self," it goes on to explain how that when we attach to and completely identify with these conditions, we create a construct of ourselves that we believe to be fixed and permanent. By doing this, we don't see the temporary nature of those conditions, and thus, the impermanence of the construct.

We do not understand that our attachment to this fixed idea of ourselves is based on these temporary conditions, and that this keeps us stuck in pursuing and avoiding the conditions as we try to make this idea of ourselves happy and comfortable. We cannot see that what we are actually doing is remaining stuck in our identification with what we think about our existence, rather than living in a real-time, present moment of how we truly do exist.

The more we pursue and avoid these conditions as we attempt to find pleasure and avoid pain, the more we get stuck in them, which in turn causes us even more struggle. Or better put, we turn our pain into suffering. It's not easy, as we often will stumble. But it's alright to stumble; we all do! Just don't get angry at yourself when you do.

So how do we have a personal, unique experience of this self that doesn't really exist? The answer is to let go of our belief in the construct of self that we have created and grab on tightly to emptiness.

The true irony of this struggle is that while practitioners swear that they want to be liberated and to transform, they do not see the problem with their trying to transform and be liberated from what they believe to be fixed and permanent. They spend a lot of time and wasted energy "working" on a self that can't be worked on. And ironically it's the doing of this "work" that keeps the problem self-perpetuating, as the work rather than eliminating the problem, actually keeps it present and makes it worse by keeping us stuck in it! A Zen koan speaks to this:

> A student said to Bodhidharma, "Please pacify my angry mind!"
> Bodhidharma replied, "Show me your angry mind."
> "I can't," the student said. "I'm not angry right now."
> "There," Bodhidharma smiled, "your mind is pacified."

Hopefully, you're not angry about all of this, and I've pacified your mind on this subject! If so, then you are now ready to be briefed on the next aspect of being the Buddha's bodyguard, which is to understand *how* a threat begins.

4

The Second Noble Tactical Truth

"There Is a Beginning to Suffering"

Security Breach – There Is a Beginning of a Threat

The Buddha's Second Noble Truth states that there is a beginning to suffering, and that it is attachment; that to guard our inner Buddha, we must understand this fact and be able to identify this starting point.

Like the bodyguard responding to a security breach, our ability to see that our mental and emotional security has been threatened or breached usually begins only after the fact that it has already been breached. And just as realizing that there has been a security breach is the first step of being safe and secure, identifying one's mental and emotional vulnerability is the beginning of eliminating it.

People most often come to Buddhism motivated by some sort of crisis, as a means of trying to understand it and find a way to deal with it, not understanding that their realization that there *is* a crisis is, in fact, dealing with it. As a master once said, "People who are looking for spirituality do not realize that they already have it." In other words, they don't see that the looking itself *is* what they are looking for; the desire to pursue a deeper level *is* a deeper level.

For bodyguards, the greatest threat is the one that is unidentified, and as I've said, more often than not, a threat is not identified until it begins. So since a security breach reveals the beginning of a threat, the first thing a bodyguard does when a client expresses their concerns about themselves and their family's safety is to do a security survey. A security survey will help identify the conditions that may create a threat and will also expose the vulnerabilities that create the opportunity for security to be breached by the threat.

This security survey involves getting extremely personal with the client and going over all aspects of their life, down to the smallest detail. Schedules, itineraries, activities, locations and the routes to and from them, and health issues, are all closely scrutinized, as well as the status of all their relationships, including family, spouses, and significant others, both current and former business associates, friends, employees, and caretakers. The client is even pressed to reveal unflattering information in regards to extramarital affairs and unethical and even illegal activities, as these are often the basis of threat vulnerability.

Once identified, these vulnerabilities are secured by altering the client's interaction with them or eliminating them altogether from the client's life. In the protection world, this is called "hardening the target."

In Buddhist practice, we must do the same thing to protect our inner Buddha. We must "harden ourselves" as targets by doing a survey of our vulnerabilities. We must get extremely personal with ourselves and ask some tough questions about our lives. We must find where our weaknesses lie, and identify what and who are threats to them. Who are the difficult people in our lives? What are the scenarios that accompany our involvement with them? What is the nature of the relationship's conditioning? What are the habitual behaviors resulting from that conditioning? What new strategy can be utilized in facing this threat, or should it be avoided entirely?

In the protection world, the question of whether to face a threat or not is often asked, as the decision to knowingly enter into a potential threat scenario must be based upon weighing the risks of doing so. This might seem like an odd question to have to ask, but many high-profile clients have responsibilities that often cannot be left unattended—to do so is nearly impossible, regardless of the bodyguard's recommendations. Many times, protection agents are undermined by clients who veto their requests to change schedules, cancel appearances, avoid certain routes, or not engage in spontaneous activity that's not on the itinerary.

The bodyguard is a detail-oriented micro-manager who, to the best of their ability, leaves nothing to chance. While the client is often short-sighted, acting on impulse, ignorant of the potential consequences of the chain of events they are setting in motion, the bodyguard relies on clearly seeing the big picture. Most times, rather than having the luxury of time to weigh the risks of an action, and being able to avoid it, if necessary, the bodyguard finds himself having no choice but to engage the risk, due to a lack of willingness and cooperation on the client's part to agree to an alternative plan.

THE TWELVE LINKS OF THE CHAIN OF CAUSATION

The Buddhist teachings of *dependent origination* and the Twelve Links of the Chain of Causation explain how our inner Buddha's safety is at risk in much the same way by detailing the process of attachment.

Dependent origination states that all things are mutually dependent—they only arise in relation to each other. A traditional teaching explains dependent origination by simply saying:

If this exists, that exists; if this ceases to exist, that also ceases to exist.

The Twelve Links of the Chain of Causation explain the workings of dependent origination by detailing the specific causes and effects that act and react to bring things into existence. These teachings go hand in hand with an understanding of the Five Aspects of Conditionality that I discussed earlier, as understanding the phenomenon that we call "self" and how its conditioned mental process works is imperative to understanding how to end suffering.

The first link in the chain is *ignorance*. The teachings define ignorance as the root of all harm and explain it as a lack of insight that is the basis of our unwholesome intention.

This ignorance leads us to the second link in the chain, which is *formation*. Formation is the coming together of our intentions, ideas, and impulses, which form our harmful thoughts, speech, and actions.

This creates the third link in the chain, which is *consciousness*. Consciousness is the awareness that results when one of the senses reacts to external phenomena.

This awareness is of the fourth link, which is *form*. Awareness of form is the recognition of sense objects and mental functions as the "self."

This recognition brings our attention to the fifth link, *senses.* The teachings refer to the functioning of self via our senses, namely our eyes, ears, nose, tongue, body, and mind.

The senses are defined as the doors through which we make *contact*, which is the sixth link. The contact it describes is of the material world.

This contact creates a response within us that leads to a more acute focus on the object of contact that is creating the stimulation, which leads to the seventh link, *sensation*. Sensation is defined as a feeling experience of the object in mind and body.

This feeling experience can be pleasant or unpleasant and creates the eighth link, *craving*. Craving is our desire for, or our aversion to the object.

This craving causes a pursuit or avoidance of the object, which leads to the ninth link, *grasping*. Grasping is the attachment or aversion actions that we take.

Grasping leads to the tenth link, *becoming*. Becoming is when we experience and internalize the results of the actions we have taken.

This internalization, often characterized by regret, matures into the eleventh link, **Birth**.

Birth is the fruition of the internalization of our actions into regret and self-loathing.

Birth leads to the twelfth and final link, **Death**. Death is the last link in the chain and the point at which the pain of our regret and self-loathing becomes suffering.

This teaching is vital, as understanding it is imperative for us to escape the repetitive cycle of our harmful conditioning. Like a hostage who with painstaking resolve diligently waits for his captors to provide a momentary window of opportunity for escape, we must be diligent with our awareness, so that we too can exploit the opportunity to escape our bondage.

Our liberation from these shackles comes from our ability to recognize and seize that ever-so-brief moment between the links when we can break the chain. Ironically, breaking free from the chain is actually the result of what we *don't* do, as we must utilize our effort to stand strong and be steadfast in refraining from our habitual reactions that keep the chain locked. We must recognize that in the moment of transition from one link to the next, rather than mindlessly grabbing the next link, we have the opportunity to *not* engage it.

The Buddha discovered this by investigating the chain in a backward succession, whereby he clearly saw that each link was the result of the one before, and the one before that, and so on.

Through this investigation he had perhaps his greatest insight: he saw that to break this cycle and end our suffering, we must refrain from acting out our habitual tendencies, which would have us cling to what is pleasant, avoid what is unpleasant, or be indifferent to what is neutral. This fundamental realization is at the foundation of how to actively live a middle way.

The following story offers an example of this chain of events. It is a composite of the actions of those involved in the situation, rather than just one individual's, but I think you'll get the gist.

I was once doing a protective detail for a television news personality who was covering the New York Yankees World Series victory parade. My partner and I were tasked to escort the reporter and his cameraman as they walked through the mob of a crowd that lined the streets. Everything went fine until we were actually done and sitting in the news van, waiting to leave *(ignorance)*. Cleanup of the thousands of pounds of confetti littering the street had begun, when suddenly, a garbage truck packed with it suddenly erupted in a huge fireball.

Seeing this, the reporter said excitedly, "There's a story!" *(formation)*. "I need to cover this!" the reporter screamed, as he jumped out of the van and yelled for his cameraman to follow him *(consciousness)*.

The reporter and cameraman both ran toward the burning truck. My plea to stop fell on deaf ears, leaving my partner and I with no choice but to jump out and run after them *(form)*.

As my partner and I ran after them I was thinking that we needed to evacuate them, as I could see the fire getting worse and smell the noxious smoke of the burning paper and garbage *(senses)*.

Getting to the location, I saw that not only was the back of the garbage truck engulfed in flames but flaming confetti and garbage were floating out of it and over the street. It didn't take long for the street, which was already completely covered in a thick coat of confetti paper, to go up in flames as well. The fire was extremely hot, and thick smoke as well as the smell of burning paper and garbage was burning our eyes and choking us *(contact)*.

The severity of the situation made me fearful for our safety, while the reporter was happy about the story *(feeling)*. I assessed that we needed to evacuate, but the reporter was moving closer to the fire, intent on getting better film for the story *(craving)*.

The reporter ignored my repeated requests to move and defiantly moved closer, then stood being filmed, with his back to the edge of the flaming street *(grasping)*.

As my partner and I jumped around, grabbing flaming debris from the air as it floated close to the reporter, we ruined several takes as we kept falling into the camera's view *(becoming)*.

The reporter said he wanted a shot of himself finishing the story by the burning garbage truck and started to walk toward it, but I grabbed his arm and stopped him *(birth)*.

He angrily berated me for stopping him *(death)*.

THE FIVE HINDRANCES

While ignorance is the leader of dependent origination and its chain of causation operation, it is supported by co-conspirators who carry out its subversive mission. While I like calling them "threats," traditional Buddhist teaching calls them the Five Hindrances and identifies them as:

1. Desire
2. Aversion
3. Restlessness
4. Sleepiness
5. Doubt

THE FIVE COUNTERMEASURES

Buddhism teaches that there are five basic countermeasures to thwart these threats, and as a result, eliminate ignorance and the behavior caused by ignorance. **The countermeasure to *desire* is satisfaction in the way things are.** This does not mean that we should not desire what we do not have. It means that we must not be attached to that desire and lose any appreciation or gratitude for what we already have, and that we should not be consumed with pursuing that desire at the expense of our equanimity.

While desire deals with our want and our attempt to fulfill that want, aversion is our response to what we perceive as harmful or negative acts that are being inflicted upon us. I say "negative acts that are being inflicted upon us," because our aversion is usually rooted in our subjective perception that we are being "done wrong"—our perception of being "done wrong" covers everyone and everything, from a random person to the whole big, bad universe itself singling us out for attack. Aversion can seem to be a justified resistance to our perception of being done wrong; however, it causes us harm because it stops us from dealing with the real issue by keeping us focused on *our* reaction rather than the cause. Ironically, later on, we often qualify most of the negative acts "inflicted upon us" as the most beneficial growth experiences of our practice.

The harm our resistance causes is twofold. We not only lash out in anger and hatred toward the situation and those we blame for it but also harshly judge ourselves and wallow in self-pity. These aversionary tactics keep us from investigating *why* we feel vulnerable and *why* we are being triggered, which in turn keeps us from beginning to heal those issues.

The countermeasure to *aversion* is acceptance. This does not mean that we condone what's happening in our lives. It means that we must not *avoid* it but face and engage the experience without attachment to our pain, and without adding paralyzing traits of resistance, such as anger and self-pity, which keep us stuck and turning pain into suffering.

The countermeasure to *restlessness* is mindfulness. Restlessness is defined as the inability to be present, rest, or relax in the moment as a result of our anxiety or boredom. This is not to say that mindfulness is simply focusing on something else as a distraction skillfully applied, as mindfulness does not involve avoiding our restlessness but instead, focusing our complete attention on it. The Buddhist newbie might think that being more aware of our restlessness will make us more restless, but the experienced practitioner understands that by investigating our restlessness we gain insight into it, and that insight gives us the wisdom to engage it, manage it, lessen it, and ultimately eliminate it.

As a result, we learn that the purpose of mindfulness is to deconstruct experience to its most basic conditioned level, and in doing so, we experience the non-self, impermanence, and suffering. I'll discuss mindfulness in more detail in the chapter titled "The Buddha's Eightfold Tactical Plan," but the focus of mindfulness in this context is to show us the temporary conditions that make up our restlessness.

Rather than identifying with and attaching to the subjective thoughts of "*I* am restless" or "*I* am bored," we understand that restlessness and boredom are simply experiences that are present; the temporary conditions on which they depend for their reality are subject to change, and so too will our experiences. We also see that if we do not attach to them, we can change by letting the conditions change, or by taking action to change them.

This reminds me of the old cliché, "If you are bored, it's because *you* are boring!" While at first glance this just seems like a funny statement, when we truly investigate experiences like boredom and restlessness, we clearly see how we are both the *cause* and the *solution*.

The countermeasure to *sleepiness* is concentration. The hindrances are often discussed in relation to seated meditation. In that context, sleepiness is to be understood exactly at face value: the problem of lacking energy or falling asleep during meditation practice. But when we expand the definition to include the context of a meditative life, it refers to our being lazy in our practice, of choosing to *not* do the things we know that we need to do. So in this context, concentration moves from simply focusing on staying awake to creating intention for how we need to act, as well as energizing our motivation to act.

The countermeasure to *doubt* is patiently conducting surveillance and assessing the validity of our doubt. There are two aspects to doubt: the first is that we doubt the practice itself, and the second is that we doubt our ability to do the practice. Since Buddhism isn't a practice that requires a belief in a deity, unlike most religions (while I don't consider my Buddhism a religion, many do), it actually urges us *to* doubt, rather than identifying doubt as a flaw or defect in the practitioner and then using it as a way of coercing them into blindly following a belief system. On the contrary, Buddhism urges us to investigate our subjective direct experience, and based on that investigation that we should draw our own conclusions and from those conclusions cultivate our actions.

As the Buddha said, "Be a lamp unto yourself and find your own way." Tactical Dharma directs us to do the same. It is each Buddhist operative's directive to harden themselves as targets. Doing a security survey and identifying vulnerabilities exposes the chain of triggers that initiates the threats of suffering we face. We must be diligent in securing our vulnerabilities, as our enemies are always near, waiting for the right moment to infiltrate and attack. So let's take a look at the defensive tactics laid out in the Third Noble Tactical Truth on how to avoid being ambushed by these near enemies.

5

THE THIRD NOBLE TACTICAL TRUTH

"THERE IS AN END TO SUFFERING"

Threat Management – There Is an End to the Threat

In protection work, a client's safety is dependent on threat management, or better put, managing vulnerabilities and opportunities
so that threats cannot be successfully executed. Threat management is
mostly about protecting the client from themselves, and it's no different
in Buddhist practice, as no matter how difficult our lives get due to our
outside problems, our biggest threat is *always* ourselves and what's going
on *within* us.

In Buddhism, the Third Noble Truth says that there is an end to suffering, and that this end comes with breaking our attachment. This does
not mean that there is an end to pain; it means that we learn how to not
turn our pain into suffering.

So, just as the bodyguard manages a threat, in order to guard our
inner Buddha we must learn to manage our pain. We do this not by
responding with either attachment or avoidance to any type of pursuit
but by managing our vulnerabilities and not providing the opportunity
for threats to successfully execute the attacks that cause our attachments.

This starts with understanding the subtle ways that desire and aversion can be exploited by our enemies against us. As I mentioned earlier, there are always enemies nearby who are infiltrating our defenses.
It is imperative that we root out these covert double agents embedded
within us. Like a terrorist sleeper cell, our harmful conditioning lies in

wait, looking for the opportunity to strike. Once activated, it triggers unwholesome thoughts, which give orders to its undercover operatives to carry out subversive, unskillful actions that cause horrific casualties in our lives. These double agents are masterful character assassins, spies who are hiding in plain sight disguised as our greatest allies.

THE FOUR QUALITIES OF ENLIGHTENMENT AND THEIR NEAR ENEMIES

We think that we are safely surrounded by a protective detail made up of the Four Qualities of Enlightenment: Lovingkindness, Compassion, Sympathetic Joy, and Equanimity. What we don't realize is that all is not as it seems, as we are about to be betrayed by the undercover operatives that Buddhism calls the "near enemies."

The near enemies are secret agents whose code names are Attachment, Pity, Envy, Insincerity, and Indifference. These agents infiltrate our security by using the Qualities of Enlightenment as their disguises.

These double agents have embedded themselves within our protective detail and are using it as their cover. As they are secret agents, they are able to carry out their espionage with a smoke-and-mirrors operation that goes undetected, because its characteristics are sinisterly similar to what we experience via the Four Qualities of Enlightenment. Because they simulate the same resulting feelings, we mistake it as the same healthy experience, when in fact it is the exact opposite. We don't see this because the experience feels so familiar we automatically trust it, which enables these double agents to get close enough to take us out.

Too over the top with the cloak-and-dagger speak? Maybe, but metaphor aside, it really is *that* devious and *that* serious. The consequences are devastating when we mistake our enemies for our allies, as they subvert our dharma operation by orchestrating an experience that at first seems nourishing but ends up poisoning us.

I'll now brief you on how to detect when the near enemies have infiltrated your operation.

Love versus Attachment

The old cliché that describes a person as someone who "loves to be in love" describes this near enemy's operation perfectly. This is exactly the dynamic of how this near enemy operates, as what feels like love actually turns out to be the acting out of unhealthy, harmful attachment. And while we might engage in actions that are perceived by others as loving, what we are really doing is acting out our desire to fulfill our own selfish needs. While these actions and the feelings that rise from them might feel the same as when one truly is acting out of love, the intentions behind them are contradictory.

Compassion versus Pity

The dynamic of this near enemy's operation is that while we feel like we are being compassionate, and our actions appear to be compassionate, rather than acting from an intention of caring for the benefit of another, we are really just acting out of pity for another in order to benefit ourselves.

Sympathetic Joy versus Envy

The dynamic of this near enemy's operation is that while we feel like we are acting out of happiness for another's success, what we are really doing is just riding their coattails for our own benefit, selfishly enjoying the fruits of their success as a way to remedy our envy and resentment of it.

Equanimity versus Indifference

The dynamic of this near enemy's operation is that while we feel like we are experiencing equanimity, and our actions appear to demonstrate that we are finding a healthy balance in our acceptance of things, the truth is that what we are really doing is avoiding dealing with our issues by having convinced ourselves that we do not care.

RENUNCIATION PRACTICE

Since the near enemies attack us by corrupting the intent behind our actions, most often our greatest security, the most tactical countermeasure we can utilize in threat management, is to be found in what we *don't* do. As I've already mentioned, in protection work this is part of what we call "hardening the target"; in Buddhist practice, it is called renunciation practice.

Just as "hardening the target" simply means that we make the target harder to threaten by identifying its vulnerabilities and the opportunities to threaten them, renunciation practice involves eliminating our vulnerabilities and the opportunities to exploit them by breaking our attachment to harmful thoughts and actions.

A Buddhist teacher once said, "we must do *not doing*." To *do* not doing, we must consciously refrain from engaging in those harmful mindsets and actions.

The five basic conduct commitments of *doing not doing*, also known as the Renunciation Tactics of Buddhism, are:

1. **Do not kill**
2. **Do not steal**
3. **Do not misuse speech**
4. **Do not misuse sexuality**
5. **Do not misuse intoxicants**

These are actually not mandates but rather a guideline of moral and ethical actions to be subjectively determined by each practitioner. Most people who are new to practice read them at face value and understand them as: Do not murder, do not rob a bank, do not lie, do not force or coerce someone to have sex or cheat on your significant other, and do not get drunk or high. They then immediately think that they have this Buddhist thing down because they don't do any of those things. But true Buddhist conduct practice is investigating the subtleties of these issues.

To not kill could mean becoming a vegetarian or vegan, or to support a friend and not "kill" their dream.

To not steal could mean to not "steal" extra time from work on your lunch hour or "steal" the moment from someone else. Rather than looking at not stealing as merely "not taking what's not ours," not stealing could be viewed from a perspective of being generous and as a practice of giving.

To not misuse speech, rather than simply being viewed in the context of not to lie, say hurtful things, or have idle, useless conversation, it could also be a practice of not staying silent when something needs to be said. And of course in typical contradictory Zen Master Speak, wise speech always starts with how well we *listen*.

To not misuse sexuality, rather than just being about sex, it could be a practice of treating all beings with respect or becoming an activist and fighting for gender equality or LGBT rights.

To not misuse intoxicants, rather than being understood as only refraining from drugs and alcohol, it could be viewed from the perspective of being a practice of being mindful and intentionally turning toward, and engaging in, what's painful as opposed to looking to something to use to avoid feeling that pain (which could be anything, not just drugs and alcohol).

However we each define Buddhist conduct, when we *do not doing*, we weaken the conditioned relationship and habitual reactivity in regard to the situation we are facing. This is an ongoing process and requires patience, as we cannot quickly undo years and years of deeply held beliefs and the habitual harmful behaviors that stem from them. Like a bodyguard creating the physical muscle memory of executing protection tactics by constantly training in them, to guard our inner Buddha we must create the tactical ability to refrain from doing things by repetitively exercising it. This addresses both the mental and physical aspect.

Sometimes, our harmful actions are preceded by overt harmful thinking, and sometimes we suddenly find ourselves in the midst of harmfully acting out with seemingly no internal warning at all. Whether we break attachment at the initial moment of engagement with our first harmful thought, or if we are minutes, hours, days, weeks, months, even years into acting it out, any time we do break attachment is an important moment. It is deeply beneficial, as it not only weakens our harmful conditioning in that moment but also strengthens the resolve and ability to do so in the future. (More on this later, when I discuss karma.)

The bodyguard expects things to go wrong and considers the ability to react appropriately and save the client from a sudden, unexpected near-tragedy a sign of a diligent, well-trained, well-prepared agent. So, too, in guarding our inner Buddha, we must expect unforeseen adversity and regard merely surviving it the best way we can in that moment as a sign of huge success!

It would be great if every time a bodyguard successfully protected a client everything went according to the plan, like it was right out of the "bodyguard handbook," but that's just not the case. In fact, many times, not only does it *not* go as planned but it goes horribly wrong! Most people would think that a bodyguard showing up at a safe-house with a terrified, bleeding, injured client would be considered an operation failure, but a live, safe client is always the end goal, no matter how that end goal is reached or what tactics were utilized in reaching it.

It's no different when it comes to protecting our inner Buddha! Of course, we would all love to handle our difficulties in the holiest, loftiest

Buddhist way, from right out of the "Buddhist handbook," but many times, the best we can do is save our inner Buddha's ass any way we can! A beaten, damaged Buddha surviving an attack and making it to the safe-house of the zendo (meditation center) is much, much better than *not* surviving! As the Buddha famously said, "Better to be pissed off than pissed on!" (Okay, maybe he didn't say it exactly like that!)

The reality of practice is that sometimes the best we can do is to survive by biting our lip, gritting our teeth, and not saying something terribly hurtful. Or by clenching our fists and white-knuckling it, so that we don't pick something up and throw it or knock somebody out! Maybe, at times, we should be satisfied that the best we can do is to punch the wall instead of a person. Perhaps storming out in silence is better than staying put in a loud rage, saying horrible things we will regret and never be able to take back!

Many times, I've had to resort to at least *not* doing the wrong thing so that I didn't make things horribly worse! While I wish I could be a "better" Buddhist when this happens, I definitely know that it's better to weaken my harmful conditioning a tiny, tiny bit in a healthy way, rather than adding to it in a large, unhealthy way.

So, let go of what you think about *how* a Buddhist should act, and do what you have to do when things are overwhelming you. And when it comes to putting the Buddhist teachings into action in your life, don't get discouraged if sometimes the best you can do is just a little bit better than doing your worst, which is still much better than actually doing your worst!

And speaking of our worst: Rather than viewing ourselves with disdain when we don't act as "Buddhist" as we'd like, I think it is vital to realize that the characteristics and behaviors we most often identify as our worst are rooted in instinctive survival tactics that have become deeply ingrained in the course of human evolution; that is, as a result of our repetitive behaviors over an extremely long period of time, survival instincts have become part of our biological process. At one time they were necessary for our survival; today, they simply are no longer relevant in our modern world.

The difficulty we encounter when we try to change our relationship to these ingrained behaviors is that they stem from our "survival of the fittest" mindset, where they are perceived as acts of self-empowerment and strength. So, when we try to abandon them, we struggle with the perception—from ourselves and others—that we are acting out of weakness. This response is embedded in our DNA; to *not* exhibit weakness is fundamental to our survival skills.

Our survival instincts challenge us in two problematic ways: *how* they operate, and our *response* to how they operate.

On the first point, our survival instincts trigger an immediate emotional response in us, which, in turn, triggers an immediate reaction from us. At one time, it was essential that we react without thinking twice, as our very lives depended on it; however, in a modern world, this attachment to immediate, habitual reactivity leads to grave harm—to ourselves and others—and is ultimately the reason we suffer.

It's important to note that I am not discounting the importance of our instincts and the role they play in our lives today. What I am addressing here is the harm caused by the manner in which we've been conditioned to react to these instincts.

This brings me to the second reason they are so challenging to work with. When we are triggered, our habitual response is based in an outdated, harmful, self-cherishing state of mind, in which we are willing to do anything, even harmful things. At one time, this was in the name of our survival; now, it is in the name of fulfilling our selfish desires.

That said, practice is not about trying to eradicate our survival instincts or ignore them; it is grounded in *changing our relationship* to them and learning how to utilize them in a healthy way. Rather than having a knee-jerk reaction when our survival instincts are triggered, and rushing haphazardly into a situation or panicking and avoiding it, we can utilize these reactions as moments of opportunity, times when we pause and investigate our impulses, especially the intentions behind them.

When we struggle to do the "right" thing, it is not a moral deficiency; it is a struggle to break this attachment and go against our ingrained tendencies, which are being triggered by those ancient survival instincts.

Keep in mind that what makes this struggle so difficult is that we are using a contemplative, critical thinking process to create the intention, and in turn the effort, to thwart what is in our genes, in our biology, as a deeply rooted nervous system reaction. Critical thinking is an essential tool, but it is not to be confused with being caught up in what we *think* about the situation; rather, it is a way to gain acute insight into a situation, one that allows us to *not* get caught up in thinking about it and swept away in the habitual reaction that follows. This reaction, which manifests in an adrenaline dump, is what causes the fight-or-flight response in us, which in a Buddhist context, we can call, the "pursue" or "avoid" response.

The "pause" I mentioned earlier relates to our ability to think critically, even in the throes of an overwhelming, adrenaline-fueled surge of emotional and physical stimulation, to gain the acute insight that will allow us to refrain from taking action until we have assessed the situation and decided on a wise, appropriate, and skillful response. To pause is to rest in a meditative moment, and is what is cultivated on the meditation cushion when one begins Buddhist practice.

Most practitioners are dismayed by their first meditative experience, as they have imagined a much deeper, mind-altering experience, rather than the scattered and frantic racing of the mind that actually happens in beginning meditation. What they don't realize is that this encounter with the frantic mind in basic meditation is necessary. Not only does it introduce them to the fundamental mental discipline required to deal with this mind state, and initiate a skillful action in response, but it is also the key that will open the door to the deeper meditative experiences they are seeking.

The challenge for new meditators, as noted, is that they expect to easily get into those deep meditative experiences and are shocked when they experience how active their mind is and how difficult it is to work with. Many new meditators become discouraged when they realize the hard work that will be required of them in this new practice and the long road ahead of them. Usually their problems stem from misunderstanding the goal of meditation—it is not to stop thinking but to learn how not to get swept away in thinking. Once this subtle difference is understood, it becomes easier to let thoughts come and go without adding a narrative.

This is the important first step in breaking attachment and developing an applicable skillset of the Buddha's teachings, but it's still just the first step. The Buddha said, "When I sit, I'm aware that I am sitting; when I lie down, I'm aware that I am lying down; when I stand, I am aware that I am standing; and when I walk, I am aware that I am walking." He urged us to get off the cushion and cultivate a meditative mind during *all* of our experiences.

WALKING MEDITATION

With this in mind, the next step in cultivating our meditative ability starts by adding *distractive adversity* to the scenario and involves moving from seated meditation to walking meditation in order to learn how to integrate a meditative mind into an activity less conducive to it.

One would think this would be a simple exercise, but it takes a lot of walking to learn *how* to just walk when you are walking! Walking meditation adds the extra external issues of obstacles on the path as well as the interaction with others as you walk.

I don't mean that you are training to be a "ninja warrior" on an obstacle course! By obstacles, I first mean the mental issues of being self-conscious, as well as the judgmental aspect that arises within us as we walk. It's amazing how something like walking—a movement that we do practically every minute of every day without a second thought—becomes an arduous task when we bring our attention to it. Suddenly, we find ourselves being distracted by thinking about *how* to walk, as we struggle to take a single step "correctly" without teetering from side to side and losing our balance, while at the same time worrying if anyone saw us struggling to keep our balance!

Then we find that we are struggling with judging how *other* people are walking. Our minds race as we cringe from noticing how others are out of step with the leader, or how they are going too slow or too fast. And finally, to add more difficulty to the experience, the path itself becomes the obstacle, as navigation around objects that need to be avoided or challenging terrain threatens our stability, both physically and mentally. These are all inhibiting factors that further test our ability to stay mindful, as we strive to replicate the meditative mind we have experienced on the cushion in a less conducive environment.

Two moments stand out in my own personal experience of learning these lessons. Both came while working with my first teacher, Noah Levine.

The first was at a day retreat that Noah held at Tibet House in New York City, where he had us doing walking meditation through a room filled with glass showcases that housed rare Tibetan artifacts. I'll never forget the anguish I experienced as I nervously navigated through that maze. I felt like a bull in a china shop! And even though, intellectually, I knew that I was always a safe distance from them, my racing mind and my attachment to it had me terrified that I was about to face-plant into one of the display cases and slash my face to ribbons as the glass broke and that the priceless artifact would be destroyed! Fortunately, it was all in my mind, and I didn't damage Tibet's history!

The second experience was at another day retreat with Noah, where he had us do walking meditation through the streets of the Lower East Side of New York City. What an experience it was to walk slowly with my hands in gassho position (a traditional Zen position for the hands during walking, which is to place left fist over the solar plexus just under the ribs with the right hand placed over covering it) through the loud, fast-paced craziness that is the Bowery, as people stared, laughed, and cursed at me. My first distraction was noticing the irony of walking like a monk past CBGB's where, over 20 years earlier, I had done quite a bit of, let's just say, *not* so Buddhist stuff!

But that's another story! So let's move on!

Work Practice

The next way to evolve on our meditative path is through work practice. Work practice—usually cooking, cleaning, and sweeping—creates further adversity by having us perform a task that requires us to have an inner focus on executing it, an outward focus on the results of that execution, all while dealing with our racing mind and maintaining an awareness of all sorts of other outside distractions and obstacles.

My most poignant work practice experience came in a Tibetan center. I was asked if I would take over the setting up of the altar prior to meditation practice. Now don't picture your little home altar. This was a 15-foot-long and 5-foot-wide shrine that was adorned with statues, candles, incense, pictures, flowers, and numerous bowls and glasses that were filled with everything from water, yogurt, and believe it or not, Jack Daniels (though I never really got a clear understanding of why, other than it had something to do with some secret, advanced tantra practice that I wasn't involved with).

Anyway, while most practitioners considered this job an honor, as to do it would put the person at the top of the work hierarchy, I wanted absolutely nothing to do with it. Being as anti religious ritual as I was, it was a miracle I was even meditating and listening to dharma talks at this center in the first place, so hell would have to freeze over before I would agree to take part in the ritual trapping that was setting up a shrine! I swore that there was no way that I would be trapped by trappings. . .

Which, in the end, is why I agreed to do it, as deep down I knew that going against my resistance would greatly benefit my practice. I knew that taking on the work would aid in my ability to thwart attachment; what I didn't expect was not only would I end up enjoying it but it would deeply change my perspective on traditional rituals, in general.

By breaking my attachment to the anti-religious conditioning that had caused my resistance and changing my fixed view, I freed myself to find value in all rituals. I had been stuck in viewing these types of rituals as useless endeavors that fortified belief in supernatural, metaphysical practices aimed at deity worship and experiencing other realms. While this was of no interest to me in my own practice, I found that I could use those same rituals as an engaged meditative practice in the here-and-now.

So I approached the task of setting up the altar in the same way as I approached doing sitting meditation on the cushion. I decided that I would light the candles and incense, fill all the bowls and glasses perfectly level to the rim without spilling a drop, arrange the flowers, place the pictures, and do prostrations mindfully but without adding a narrative or being swept away by a random thought—I would use it as an exercise in being completely present.

At the time I was also attending a Zen center. Similarly, I found that rather than viewing the chanting and liturgy as something to be avoided or "put up with" to get to the meditation, dokusan (private koan study), and dharma talks, I could use them as an engaged meditation activity, just as I did with the altar ritual at the Tibetan center. So, while the guy next to me was chanting for the purpose of honoring the Zen ancestors and gaining merit for his future reincarnation into his next life, I was simply doing it as a way of being fully engaged and present and embodying the ritual for its duration.

I began to apply this perspective to every task in my life, no matter how mundane and distasteful, and to every Buddhist ritual I had disdain for, such as bowing, prostrations, and banging gongs and wooden fish. And while this did not make every task I was resistant to suddenly enjoyable, it sure kept them from being the torture they once were, or better put, it kept me from torturing myself over them.

Ironically, this experience was one of the most valuable lessons I ever learned in practice, because since then, I've found that almost all of my transformation has been due to my doing the things I don't want to do! Even now, if I am searching for an answer and trying to clarify what action to take, I often look to the *opposite* of my first inclination and do that.

Work practice is vital, as it is the closest we can come in training to simulating real life experience within the zendo, but since it is a controlled environment, we are not truly learning to develop a realistic application of mindfulness. This brings me to my next point, which is that the only way to develop realistic application of the teachings and integrate a meditative mind into our "real" lives *is* to integrate a meditative mind into our "real" lives! What I mean by this is that we have to get out there and put it to the test under circumstances that are least conducive, as the more we do this the better we will get at doing it.

The only way we will truly learn to implement the "pause" *is* to pause. The only way we can learn to appropriately use our survival instinct *is* to use our survival instinct. And the only way we can survive in the midst of overwhelming adversity that threatens our survival *is* to face overwhelming adversity that threatens our survival!

According to the Buddha, if we let our survival instincts manifest into attachment when faced with overwhelming adversity that threatens our survival, they become our greatest threats. He identified this manifestation in a general way as *greed, hate, delusion*, and in a more acute way as *desire, wanting, clinging, craving, pursuing, aversion, anger*, and *doubt*.

Where it was once necessary to use these instincts in the most selfish, extreme manner possible, as a matter of life-or-death survival, we now must liberate ourselves from the self-serving mentality they have created, which causes us to live attached to the self-cherishing concepts of *I, me,* and *mine*, and the pursuit and avoidance that arise from those mental states.

What also makes this difficult, as mentioned earlier, is the different nature of the threats we face today compared with when we were half-naked, cave-dwelling cro-magnon humans. Back then, threats were visible and easily identifiable, and the "flight-or-fight" reaction literally meant to either physically stay put and make a strong stand and fight or evacuate and take cover. In the modern world, though, our threats are not so easily assessed, as they are rooted in emotional and mental conflicts that are sometimes so subtle they can lie undetected for long periods of time. And when they are identified, they require a nuanced response, rather than a knee-jerk survival reaction that causes more harm than good.

The Buddha used a fitting metaphor in reference to changing our mentality about how we use our survival instincts: he called it going *against the stream*. By this, he not only meant that we should go against our own harmful conditioned inclination to act but also that we should fight against being mindlessly swept away by the delusions inherent in the current of life itself, which condition us in the first place.

Going *with* the stream keeps us caught in an illusion and not able to clearly see reality as it is; to "go against the stream" is to change direction, find an alternate route.

Many times in the bodyguard world, the most successful counter-measures are to retreat and evacuate via an alternate route and guard our inner Buddha. The teachings also map out our alternative route. So in the next stage of this operation, I'll brief you on this protocol.

6

THE FOURTH NOBLE TACTICAL TRUTH

"THERE IS A WAY TO END SUFFERING"

Evacuation – There Is a Route to the End of the Threat

Security details never go as planned, and the bodyguard must always be prepared to spontaneously change tactics, based on new information discovered during an ongoing threat assessment, or worse, based on the event of an attack.

Always in place is an alternate escape route, with identified safehouses to retreat to. For bodyguards, this can actually be a single, secured, covert spot, or simply having identified police stations, hospitals, or emergency response units close to the scheduled locations on the client's itinerary.

To retreat is not a mission failure, but rather a viable survival tactic, an alternate path to success. In Buddhism, we change the path we are on by "taking refuge" in the **Buddha** (the teacher), the **Dharma** (the teachings), and the **Sangha** (the community that follows the teacher and practices the teachings), then continue to do so as our ongoing survival tactics.

A protection agent evacuating a client in order to retreat from a threat is not a mission failure, and neither is a Buddhist practitioner needing to take refuge. In fact, it's the consistent starting point of our mission's success. Instead of the act of "taking refuge" being a tactic of aversion to the path, it is a commitment that makes us more securely embedded within it.

If we look at our Buddhist practice as a mission (let's say, "Operation Liberation"), then the act of taking refuge is our acceptance of the mission and making a formal commitment to carry it out. It's our taking the oath and being sworn in to the Buddhist Dharma Forces.

In doing so, we are committing to follow the Buddha's leadership example of how *he* executed *his* "Operation Liberation," and adhering to his dharma teachings as the instructional orders of his strategy in our *own* execution of the operation. The sangha then functions as support of our mission by providing a home base from which we operate, and by providing additional operatives as reinforcements to support us in completing our mission objective.

The initial briefing for our mission objective is found in the Fourth Noble Truth, which says that there is a path to the end of suffering, and that to successfully guard the Buddha we must evacuate via this alternate route. This is identified in our mission plan as the "middle way."

THE MIDDLE WAY

The middle way is our evacuation route from suffering, a clear path of navigation through life's potential ambushes. I say "potential," because ultimately it's our own rigidity and steadfastness in our attachment to our preferences and judgments that keeps us on an unsafe path that leads us directly into those ambushes.

Like the client that refuses to alter their itinerary to protect themselves, we become attached to our self-declared VIP status and refuse to be flexible about our desires. We want *what* we want *when* we want it. We want reality to conform to our idea of how we want it to be, rather than accepting the way it is—at the expense of both our own well-being and that of others.

Buddhism teaches us that there are eight potential ambush scenarios. They are:

Pain and **Pleasure**
Gain and **Loss**
Praise and **Blame**
Fame and **Disrepute**

There is no avoiding these scenarios, as we will all have to face them, regardless of our intentions and actions. So it is important to realize that these scenarios are not threats in and of themselves; what makes them potential ambush scenarios is the nature of our relationship *with* them and our habitual reactivity in response *to* them. Depending on our diplomacy in dealing with them, we can either negotiate with them to be our allies or implement policies that turn them into our adversaries.

In dealing with them, rather than arming ourselves with desire and attacking them, or cloaking ourselves in camouflage and avoiding them, our directive is that we must tactically engage them and deal with them by navigating right down the middle of them. We must hide in plain sight.

When a bodyguard plans a security detail, they must not only plan alternate evacuation routes but also identify places to evacuate to along those routes. As I mentioned earlier, police stations, firehouses, hospitals, and emergency medical squads are chosen and designated as safe spots to seek refuge. They can be utilized to proactively thwart an attack if the detail identifies the signs that one could be imminent, or to reactively evacuate to them when an attack has occurred, or to treat a medical emergency as it happens. On a lesser note, alternate routes are not only established to keep the VIP safe but also to make them more comfortable and at ease, as it provides a way to avoid protests, demonstrations, picket lines, the press, being photographed or filmed, or just simply identifying a faster route that keeps an impatient client happy.

As I've mentioned, the bodyguard's decision in taking an alternate route is not cowardly, or seen as a statement of security failure. It involves facing a situation with honesty and clarity and dealing with it head-on. What *would* be a security failure is if the bodyguard did not acknowledge the need to make changes to the detail's security plan when it is warranted.

Implementing the Buddhist teaching of "living the middle way" is no different. To be in pain is not a failure in practice but a natural part of living that needs to be faced. The middle way is not a route of avoidance; rather, it is an altered route that takes us directly into the heart of the painful situation.

I say "altered" because our old way of dealing with the issues and situations that threatened and harmed us was to avoid them at all costs. So while altering our route to meet them head-on might seem counter-productive in "protecting" our inner Buddha, the contrary is true: to meet them head-on once and for all is the only way to learn how to manage them and ultimately eliminate them. This means that we stay with the painful experience and do not go to either of its polar extremes—to avoid it and suffer over the pain or attach to pursuing bliss with the intent of using it to eliminate the pain.

Admittedly, there are times when traversing the middle way puts us in the midst of an extreme attack we aren't prepared for, and like the bodyguard protecting his client, we will also need to alter our route further. This might involve avoiding specific people or situations, breaking attachment to harmful emotional and mental extremes, or running to a fellow practitioner or the zendo for help. This is not to abandon the middle way, but to take cover along it.

Taking Refuge in the Zendo

So if the middle way explains *why* we take refuge, the zendo many times is *where* we take that refuge, as seeking safe haven within the security of our Buddhist safe-house at times can be the wisest way to ensure that our inner Buddha is kept safe.

Sometimes, just being in a secure location gives us the relief we so desperately need. Often the zendo is the middle ground that gives us a firm place to stand while walking the middle way, and evacuating to it for the security it offers, rather than staying involved in a harmful situation, can be our most viable survival tactic. This does not mean that we cannot implement the Buddhist teachings successfully; rather, it means that sometimes the best implementation of the teachings is to know when to retreat, take cover, and regroup for another offensive action.

When I teach personal protection to civilians and martial arts students, I'm frank about the fact that evacuation is always the first protocol, but if evacuation is not possible, then surviving a situation with the *least* amount of injury and trauma is the most viable outcome that one should ever realistically expect.

Most untrained people mistakenly think that learning martial arts techniques or defensive tactics will give them the skillset to easily overcome an attacker and remain unscathed, but nothing could be farther from the truth.

The reality is that most "trained" people are *not* prepared to respond realistically for a real altercation, because their "training" is simply drilling technique with a compliant partner in a manner conducive to its success. And while drilling is fundamental in developing a foundation, if the practitioner is only doing this type of training, no matter how well they are trained in drilling, they will never develop realistic application of that technique. The truth is that the only way to do so is to train the technique under realistic circumstances that are *not* conducive to it.

Now, martial artists that haven't had this insight yet will quickly defend themselves and their training by saying that through drilling they are developing the muscle memory to realistically apply it should the need arise, but I disagree. My experience has taught me that the muscle memory being developed during drilling is simply muscle memory equipped to respond to drilling; it will fail when put to the test under real circumstances.

As I said, drilling is an important place to work from in order to begin to develop a foundation that can be adapted into realistic application. The problem is that few practitioners evolve past it to do so. This doesn't mean that we should go out and get into altercations for the purpose of honing our skills for realistic application. It simply means that in training we must simulate, to the best of our ability, the stress characteristics of a real situation.

It's important to note that even when we do this to the best of our ability, while we can come very close in many respects, it still falls short of what we will experience in a real situation. The reality is that whether in a personal protection situation or in a situation of assimilating the Buddhist teachings into skillful action, how we rise to the occasion will depend upon the level of preparation we are falling back upon.

In personal protection, what we try to simulate in these training scenarios are the stress symptoms of the fight-or-flight experience. As I said earlier, we are all hardwired with this vital survival instinct, but when one is not versed in the experience of handling the adrenaline dump that accompanies the triggering of those survival instincts, it overwhelms the ability to react appropriately. That's because the stress that is experienced results in motor skill diminishment, disrupted and impaired respiration, tunnel vision, auditory exclusion, and an impaired thought process, making it impossible to properly assess the situation and respond appropriately.

This does not mean that training in the techniques while simulating the stress and duress of a real situation will automatically enable someone to learn how to have their normal, full application ability in spite of the symptoms; rather, it teaches them to expect the duress symptoms and develop an altered, appropriate application when they take place. If a response fails due to the bodyguard being under excessive stress that they have not adequately prepared for, evacuation is always taught as the most viable survival tactic.

Protecting our inner Buddha is no different. We must train ourselves to expect our skillfulness to diminish and our mindfulness to be disrupted and impaired as we apply the teachings while under the duress of life's most painful and challenging experiences. Staying grounded in the middle way depends on our ability to be able to wisely handle our fight-or-flight instinct in response to an attack on our emotional and mental state.

So if the emotional and mental extremes we face are suffering and bliss, the middle way gives us a place to stay safe in-between those two extremes; however, if our tactical dharma response fails, evacuation, whether from a difficult person or harmful situation, is both our most viable tactic and last resort.

At this point, most people respond, "I get why I would not want to suffer, but why would I not want to be blissful?" The answer is not that we do not enjoy pleasure in Buddhist practice but that pleasure taken to the extreme of bliss results in suffering as well.

To help us understand this, let's first look at what happens when we are faced with a painful experience. Avoiding the painful experience negates our ability to deal with it, which in turn compounds its harmful mental and emotional effects into suffering—we suffer not from the initial pain but from avoiding that pain. We compound this suffering by trying to prematurely end it and not letting it run its natural course. We end up stuck in what we think about it, in what we add to it, rather than facing it realistically and working through it, which would help manage and dissipate the pain, and in turn help us avoid suffering. The irony is that had we just dealt with the pain immediately, our difficulties would have been a fraction of what they became by avoiding it.

Bliss is no different. As I said earlier, to try and use bliss as a coping mechanism for pain causes suffering. While it is fine to enjoy pleasure, when it's taken to an unhealthy extreme we also suffer. This unhealthy extreme is our inability to realize that pleasurable experiences end. By not accepting that fact, we end up clinging to pleasure and unnaturally trying to prolong it, or once it has ended, we pursue it at all costs as we try to recapture or re-create it.

In both instances, we cause ourselves immense suffering. The sad irony is that not only do we have to learn how to not cling and pursue; we even have to learn to be fully present and just enjoy pleasure in the first place, as just the knowledge that it will end undermines our ability to do even that, when we are in the midst of it! We can't enjoy ourselves because we are so worried about *not* enjoying ourselves! Our inability to do so leads us to take clinging and pursuit to such a detrimental extreme.

Now that I've addressed *why* we need to follow the middle way, I'll address the tactics of executing *how* to follow it. In the bodyguard world, the first and foremost survival tool utilized by a security detail is the gathering of intelligence, and Buddha, the director of our security, also details the implementing of an intelligence-gathering strategy as the first execution of his eightfold tactical plan in fortifying our middle way route. I hope you trust in the wisdom of his orders.

7

THE EIGHTFOLD TACTICAL PLAN
EXECUTING THE BUDDHA'S
ALTERNATE ROUTE

While the middle way describes the layout of the route, the Buddha's teaching of the Eightfold Path explains how to navigate and traverse that route.

As I mentioned earlier, the first tactic of preparing a security detail is the gathering of intelligence. Likewise, in Buddhism, the first tactic of protecting our inner Buddha on the path of liberation is to cultivate wisdom.

But before I begin this briefing on executing the tactics of the path, I think it's important to point out that while, in the traditional way, the components of the path are presented with the word *right* before each one, I have purposely chosen to use the lesser-used descriptive term of *wise*.

This deliberate difference is to address an important aspect of the execution of these tactics, namely the aspect that no tactic, or the application of it, can ever be considered always to be right or appropriate. In contrast, not only is it always possible to be wise but the most important point of utilizing wisdom is to be able to use that wisdom to assess when a tactic must be modified so that its application can be adapted to a change in circumstance that has resulted from changing conditions.

With this in mind let's begin the briefing.

THE COMPONENTS OF
WISDOM PRACTICE

The first component of wisdom practice is *Wise Understanding*. In general terms, this understanding refers to an understanding of the dharma, specifically of the Four Noble Truths and the nature of suffering.

Just as the bodyguard uses the gathering of intelligence to formulate a plan, the Buddhist practitioner uses the second component of wisdom practice, *Wise Thought*, to do the same, using thinking that is rooted in wise understanding to formulate the plan of action they intend to utilize.

The intention that forms from wise understanding and wise thinking points directly to how the Buddhist practitioner must act. So the next three aspects of the route are rooted in the actions of *Wise Speech, Wise Action,* and *Wise Livelihood*—what we say, what we do, and how we earn a living.

The general understanding is that we *do not cause harm.*

This is not as easy as it sounds. We need to be rigorously honest with ourselves about our intentions. If the intentions behind our actions are not wholesome the actions we take, which we *think* are *helpful,* might actually cause *harm,* and the actions that we *think* are *harmful* and refrain from might actually have been *helpful.*

At this point, we realize that wisdom is not enough, and that we need to establish an ethical foundation for our intentions to rest upon. Buddhist teachings help us by offering a general guideline of directives to follow in regard to our conduct.

But before I talk about the basic five conduct directives, here's a story from my bodyguarding days that illustrates how what appears to be a breach of the conduct directives is actually helpful, appropriate, and skillful action when investigated based on the intention that is behind it.

For several years I was given a security detail for a major news outlet to protect a reporter and cameraman as they covered the Million Youth Marches in New York City. These events were difficult, as they were held in the streets of Harlem, which were tight and crowded, which made an already volatile situation more threatening to those involved, and severely limited our ability to evacuate, if needed.

Prior to going, my partner and I discussed our protective strategy. We knew the crowd would be predominately African American and extremely passionate about the issues being brought up by the rally speakers. We also knew that the speakers would be playing to those emotions, even attempting to exploit them.

We knew that we could be viewed negatively, not so much for being white (although it was an issue) but more for being seen as representatives of a major media outlet, as the media was viewed as being extremely biased in their reporting, and for no other reason but simply being there at all (I do remember feeling like we were trespassing, though we were simply walking public streets). We decided that if faced with any adversity, we would respond with the strategy of offering the person the chance to air their feelings on the news. We never would promise them they would be on, but we would film them and give them an opportunity to have a voice and chance to be heard.

For the most part, we walked through the crowd without incident other than the occasional insulting comment. The few times an angry person did get in our faces and angrily yelled and screamed, we responded by treating them with respect and understanding and offered them the chance to say it all on the news.

It would go something like this: First, I understood that the anger wasn't personally against me, so I would explain to them that they were wasting their time yelling at us, that we were just doing a job and that we were not against their cause, and how about getting to tell those who didn't understand or actually were against them. They went for it every time. The chance to seemingly have their say and be heard was the perfect diffusal tactic. It immediately calmed them down and gave them an outlet other than us to vent their frustration and anger at.

It might not seem like a big deal, but when you picture a small area overcrowded with thousands of frustrated, angry, and passionate people on a hot summer's day, it's a recipe for disaster—a disaster we needed to do anything and everything to avoid, as I knew that if the emotions escalated to violence, we would be in dire straits, with no easy evacuation to even a police substation set up every 50 yards or so, let alone being able to get out of there!

Needless to say, it worked perfectly! Time after time, I was able to coax an angry rally participant onto their soap box in front of the camera. I'd excitedly exclaim, "Wait! Hold that thought for the camera," as the reporter would get in position for the "interview" and tell them exactly where to stand. The cameraman would then "count it down . . . 3,2,1, go!" And with that the person would be off and running with their rant. We'd let them speak as long as they wanted, and once they were done, they not only were completely calm but even were thanking me for the opportunity and asking that I put in a good word to the producers so that their segment would be aired.

I don't know if you've guessed it or not, but since I've been talking about skillful means and doing what's appropriate in a situation, even if it's being untruthful, well, truth be told, we didn't film one person that day! We pretended to, but not one of them was actually recorded. It was all a strategic ruse to de-escalate a potentially volatile situation.

This is an important point. Buddhist teachings say that what's most important in regards to our actions is the intention behind them. Yes, I lied and manipulated that day, but the intention behind those actions was to keep people safe.

This doesn't mean that as Buddhists we can run around doing whatever we want without consequence. Actually it's the exact opposite! Buddhism teaches us that there is a consequence for every action, even if we aren't aware of it, and stresses how we must be brutally honest with ourselves about our intentions, as well as giving us exact conduct practices to follow.

And even when we follow those conduct practices and our intention is pure, it doesn't mean that we are free from consequence of those actions, as even the most virtuous act, fueled by the most pristine intention, can cause harm in some capacity. But as it turned out the rally participants were the least of our problems, so back to the story.

All the streets had been closed to traffic, and the rally area had been cordoned completely off with metal barricades. As we walked into the surrounding streets outside the rally area, I noticed many clean-cut young men dressed impeccably in suits and bow ties. I knew that this was a Nation of Islam event so I recognized them as members, like anyone else would, but I also recognized that they were strategically posted around the perimeter and walking in tight details, doing surveillance within the crowd. What I particularly noticed was how one of these guys kept his gaze on us as he lifted his hand to his mouth and spoke, cupped his ear, spoke into his sleeve again and how we were suddenly being followed.

We slowly made our way through the packed crowd to an entrance into the rally area. The entrance was a makeshift opening between two of the large metal barriers that surrounded the area, with two Nation of Islam security people standing on each side of it.

I approached with a smile and a respectful tone and said, "Excuse us, please, guys," but as I began to walk through, the guy to my left stepped in front of me to block his side of the entrance, as the guy to my right pushed the metal barrier forward to close his side of the opening, painfully slamming it on my leg as he did.

As we stood toe to toe "discussing" my team's entry into the event and his refusal to allow it, I was thankful for one of New York's "finest" intervening and ordering them out of our way. While I had been doing everything possible to calmly reason with them, the situation was getting a bit tense.

I thanked him as he moved the gate out of our way, to which he responded with a stone-cold icy stare of contempt. (Actually, I was quite impressed with the Nation of Islam security guys, as in a crowd of over six thousand of us packed shoulder to shoulder, they stood at their posts, dressed in suits, standing like statues, motionless in the sweltering summer heat of New York City.)

Emotions were tense, and tempers were at their boiling points, and the organizer of the event, Khalid Abdul Muhammad, fueled that fire by exploiting those emotions with a thinly veiled anti-white, and blatantly overt anti-police rant. While we made it through without serious incident, my partner and I took a lot of intentional pushes, shoulders, and elbows, as we escorted our reporter and cameraman through the thick crowd.

Some would say we were lucky that a situation ripe for escalation to blow up in our faces with serious, if not deadly, consequences did not. Perhaps, to an extent, we were. I firmly believe, however, that the ability to remain nonattached to the verbal insults and minor physical incidents and the skillfulness to respond calmly and appropriately with understanding and kindness (with a bit of well-intentioned deception thrown in) were the reasons we were able to keep our subjects and ourselves safe.

As I mentioned, I worked this detail for two consecutive years. The first year was far worse as regards the crowd, but while we did face a bit of the same adversity, it was much less, as was the event's attendance. And not only was the attendance less, but rather than supporting the event, many were speaking out *against* it. The second year our biggest problem actually stemmed from the reporter we were protecting, but I'll get to that in a bit.

First let me tell you a bit of the backstory that resulted in a different attitude toward us from the crowd.

It seems that, the first year, the Harlem community strongly supported the event. That tide had quickly turned when the organizer, Khalid Abdul Muhammad, after denouncing the NYPD and advocating that the community use violence against them, then used the NYPD to help escort him out of the event. Their sentiment toward him worsened further when it was later reported that he had departed in a huge, stretch limousine.

A sentiment I heard often from the second-year attendees was that they felt that he was using their community for his own selfish gain, and in the year that had passed since the first event he had not done a thing for the betterment of the Harlem community.

Muhammad must have known of this sentiment because, at the end of the second event, rather than being ushered off the back of the stage under police protection to a waiting stretch limo, he made his closing remarks ending the event and walked off the front of the stage directly into the crowd.

At the time that he did this, most of the attendees, including myself, had our backs to him and were walking away from the stage to exit, so when the crowd realized he had come down and joined them, they all turned around and rushed back toward him, as did our reporter, smelling a chance to put a microphone in his face.

My partner and I struggled as we tried to stop people from knocking the reporter or cameraman down, but to her credit (and with our help), our reporter got up close to Muhammad and began yelling questions at him.

As more and more of the crowd realized what was happening and made their way back to the stage, the situation took a turn for the worse. We were standing several feet from the stage, with nowhere to go, and more and more people surging toward us. The crowd was being pushed backwards against each other, and ultimately against the stage. It took all I had to stand rigid and protect the reporter (and myself) from being crushed, so I called for us to evacuate.

While our reporter and cameraman complied, the wall of people behind us didn't get the order, and they continued to force their way forward against us. I quickly grabbed the reporter around her waist, lifted her up in the air, and carried her, while my partner had a solid grab of the cameraman and dragged him, as we forced our way out. Several times, I came close to falling, as people were now falling and being trampled. Unfortunately, I had to step on several people who had fallen, as I made my way through the crowd carrying the reporter. After what seemed like an eternity, we finally made it out safely.

This experience was actually much more unsettling than some I have had, when I actually had to defend against an attack or fight to restrain someone, as the level of unpredictability required a level of calm and restraint in the face of it that was more difficult than actually responding to a visible, identified threat. Much like life!

Like the bodyguard scenario I just mentioned, life itself is unpredictable and at times overwhelming, even without incident. In response, Buddhist practice is not about having a steadfast code to live by, but like the bodyguard, having the ability to assess each moment subjectively, be clear about one's intention, and choose a code of conduct appropriate in the moment.

Being clear with ourselves about our intentions is vital, as without clear intention we cannot know if an act is helpful or harmful, no matter how it *appears* to be. In this case, while by lying it might appear that I was breaking the "wise speech" conduct directive, the intention behind it was to diffuse the situation and keep all involved out of harm's way. So with this in mind, let's take an in-depth look at that code of conduct.

THE FIVE CONDUCT DIRECTIVES

The five basic reactive, renunciation tactics of not to kill, not to steal, not to misuse speech, not to misuse sexuality, and not to misuse intoxicants, are the conduct tactics that will free us from our conditioned, harmful reactions and begin the liberation and transformation that we have been seeking. But important as they are, they are only part of the plan. The other strategy we implement is to be proactive and engage in mindsets and actions that will create new, helpful conditioning.

The tactics of this proactive plan are the opposite of the renunciation practices mentioned above. They direct us in a general way to:

Honor and nurture life

Rather than simply just not killing, the tactics of honoring and nurturing life are rooted in realizing the interdependence of all things and seeing that we are not separate from all that is—that not only should all beings not be harmed; they should be helped.

Use only what we need and to be generous and giving

Rather than just not stealing, to execute the tactics of using only what we need and being generous and giving requires us to hone the tactic of finding satisfaction with what we have. When we are satisfied with what we have, it frees us up from taking so that we can focus on giving to those who have less.

Use helpful speech

Rather than just not causing harm through our speech, to execute the tactic of helpful speech we must cultivate a mind that sees clearly so that we appropriately use our speech to be helpful.

Treat all people with respect and dignity

Rather than just not misusing sexuality, the tactic of treating all people with respect and dignity is executed through our ability to unconditionally accept what each moment has to offer, and involves letting go of our self-cherishing and abiding in unfulfilled desire.

Be mindful

Rather than not misusing intoxicants, executing the tactic of being mindful requires us to turn suffering into wisdom. This means that rather than turning away from difficult experience and pursuing pleasure as a way to avoid pain, we engage and experience the pain and gain insight and wisdom from the process.

THE SIX PERFECTIONS

While I will address them in much greater detail later in the book, the teachings then go on to outline a more acute directive of proactive tactical application that we need to execute, called the Six Perfections:

Generosity
Morality
Patience
Energy
Meditation
Wisdom

These more advanced proactive tactics enable us to avoid the habitual situations that give rise to the triggers that threaten us, as well as to not be triggered and to be able to safely evacuate them when we have been ambushed by them.

Again avoiding is not defined as a mission failure, nor does it mean that we do not deal with the situation we are facing. It means that because we are carrying out new healthy, wholesome tactics, we will automatically find ourselves on safer routes more of the time, and if we are ambushed and forced to detour onto a dangerous route, we are now able to handle the situation in a new, wholesome, skillful, and appropriate way.

What we *do* avoid is being a casualty. Because we are following new rules of engagement rather than just following the old, habitual orders of our conditioning, we do not end up engaging the same old enemies.

WISE EFFORT

Undoing a lifetime of harmful conditioning, and creating a completely new way of living that's in stark contrast to what one is used to is no easy task and takes an extreme amount of effort. The Buddhist teachings help us by identifying how to apply the next component of the plan: *Wise Effort*.

Most people think of effort as a singular experience, but it's important to understand that effort and its application are two different things. If we define effort as a vigorous determination or act of exertion, we can see that it describes the mental and physical intensity we engage in, but not how we *apply* that intensity.

We all have experienced the lack of result that comes from wasted energy without focus or direction. An example of this I often use while teaching martial arts is that while we all have the natural instinct and motivation to defend ourselves if we need to, the difference between a trained and untrained person is not the effort they exert in protecting themselves but how they *apply* that effort in their tactics response.

While they both will have that same basic survival instinct and adrenaline dump that I spoke about earlier in regard to the fight-or-flight instinct, a trained person will be able to focus their energy into an appropriate response that successfully thwarts the attack. The untrained person might have the same amount of energy, but it will be scattered into a panicked, erratic, frantic, flailing physicality that not only serves no purpose as an appropriate response to the threat but often puts them in greater danger as a result.

More important than the effort that is exerted is how it's directed, as effort without wisdom is a waste of our energy. So with this in mind, let's look at how the Buddhist teachings explain a wise application of effort.

They start with stating the end goals.

The Buddhist teachings continually remind us that the brain thinks. That's what it does, thinking is its purpose; therefore, we should not identify with these thoughts, as they are just a byproduct of what organically occurs.

These random trains of thought spewed by the brain can be wholesome or unwholesome, deeply significant or merely idle chatter; what makes them harmful is if we engage those thoughts and get swept away from what truly needs to be attended to in the moment. No matter how much "better" we get with our use of critical thinking, we should always expect and be prepared for the brain to do this.

By defining these trains of thought as "random," I do not mean that they are never comprised of significant issues and should always be ignored; quite the contrary. By using the word "random" in describing thoughts, I am referring to the unexpected *timing* of their arising, not their *content*.

I'll talk more about dealing with the content of thoughts later, but first, let's take a look at the four tactical applications of effort that the Buddhist teachings identify.

The Four Tactical Applications of Effort

The *first tactical application of wise effort* is to prevent entertaining and attaching to unwholesome mind states when they arise.

While sometimes we are mindful enough to see it coming and can prevent an unwholesome mind state from occurring, most times we become aware of it after the fact, so the *second tactical application of wise effort* involves breaking our attachment to the unwholesome mind state when we find ourselves stuck in it.

These first two tactical effort applications are *re*active. The next two applications are *pro*active and function on the premise that if one is engaged in a wholesome mental state, it will prevent an unwholesome one from arising. So the *third tactical application of wise effort* is to actively create a wholesome mindset.

Most of us take for granted our ability to use our minds to change our minds. So much so that it has become almost a cliché in Buddhist circles. "Change your mind" has become a buzz phrase that is thrown around as a go-to answer, but *how* to do it is rarely discussed. (There's even a "Change Your Mind Day" once a year! A mindfulness holiday so to speak.)

As we touched on earlier, the most common problem encountered by new meditators is that they misunderstand the objective of meditation and believe that why one meditates is to *stop* their thinking rather than letting their thinking happen without attaching to it. Long-term meditators understand this on a basic level, but even they fail to make the distinction between *attaching* to their thoughts and *engag*ing their thoughts.

Ironically, we must engage our thoughts to *not* be attached to them; our unwillingness to do so is rooted in our reluctance to face our issues, and is actually the attachment we are trying to avoid in the first place.

Simply put, to "attach to our thoughts" means that we get swept away in the narrative of what we add to our thoughts, thereby taking our focus away from the original thought; whereas, to "engage our thoughts" means that we stay present and use critical thinking to keep the focus on the specific thought, and *only* that thought.

This engagement can culminate in two ways. First, you can choose to stay engaged with the content of the thought and work with it. Or second, you can acknowledge that the issue needs to be dealt with but that the timing of its emergence isn't appropriate for adequate tending to and the thought can be let go of to be dealt with at a more opportune time. (More on this in a bit.)

The mental ability to do this is called "non-attached awareness" and is at the foundation of our ability to think critically. But don't confuse non-attached awareness with *detachment*. Detachment is rooted in the aversion tactic of indifference, which keeps us resistant, while non-attached awareness keeps us engaged to participate in the experience through acceptance.

While getting a handle on all this seems like an arduous task, it's really as simple as how quickly we can change our mind. So before you throw this book across the room in frustration, I'll get to the "how" of it.

The "how" of changing our mind begins with learning to use our critical thinking to both *not* attach to our random thoughts and determine what we *should* be thinking. We use non-attached awareness and critical thinking to let ourselves know that, in the midst of random thoughts, we do not have to identify with them.

We actually use the mind to see what the mind is doing and allow it to redirect itself. Once we acknowledge that our thoughts are just thoughts and not our present-moment reality, we can let them come and go, as we focus on recognizing why they are coming. The epitome of engagement without attachment is this: the ability to be completely aware of what's happening, not swept up by it, and able to use critical thinking to direct ourselves to take specific actions that not only counter the threat of attachment but ultimately eliminate it.

Now, let's get back to the issue of content.

The importance of being able to apply critical thinking lies in being able to investigate and determine that even though these thoughts are random in their timing, often their content is the result of our ingrained harmful conditioning and past trauma that needs to be dealt with. So, when these random thoughts come we don't ignore them; we acknowledge them, investigate them, and deal with them appropriately.

Sometimes, as noted earlier, the appropriate response is to simply let our thoughts pass, if our investigation determines that they are inconsequential and need no further attention. Other times, we realize that our thoughts stem from a significant issue that *does* demand our attention; however, we choose to let them go because the moment is not conducive to us dealing with them appropriately, so we will do so at a later time. And, of course, at other times, our thoughts might be so significant they demand our immediate attention, so we address them when they arise.

I've mentioned that "not attaching" means that we address the content without "adding" anything, as this additional narrative is how we attach and get stuck; however, I haven't addressed *what* it is we add that is liable to get us attached and stuck.

Traditional Buddhist teaching states that it is the pursuing and avoiding and adding content that turns what would be normal, manageable pain into excruciating suffering, so what we add is aversion, which manifests in two main ways: regret of the past or fear of the future.

When we regret the past, we relive old memories and play old mental tapes. While they might be related to the issue, they take us out of the present moment and not only hinder our ability to deal with what's happening now but actually make it worse. They harmfully compound our mental and emotional state with past pain, which further distorts and confuses our view of the issue rather than clarifying it.

When we experience fear of the future, we picture worst-case scenarios as the outcomes of our engaging and addressing the issue and feel paralyzed from taking any action; to do so, we convince ourselves, would make everything worse. It is only when we refrain from this aversion that the opportunity for us to consciously direct our critical thinking is created and we are able to start thinking differently, which in turn creates a different mindset.

The different mindset that results from our implementing the tactics of non-attached awareness and engagement creates a skillset we can use immediately to respond to the personal battles we face. This new mindset also serves our mission objective as we wage a general war on greed, hate, and delusion by either weakening our old, harmful conditioned ways of thinking or allowing a new, helpful, conditioned way of thinking to become embedded.

This is what constitutes a true "changing of the mind," as we are not simply redirecting our thinking but actually rewiring the way our brain works so that we can think in a completely different way. To say that we "rewire" how our brain works does not mean that we are merely willfully changing our thinking from one issue to another, or from being harmful to being helpful; it actually changes the neurological pathway of how the brain creates thought in the first place in a process called "neuroplasticity."

Neuroplasticity is defined as the brain's ability to alter networks of neurons, the process whereby a particular behavior creates a network of neurons, and how that network has a specific sequence of synaptic firing pertaining to that particular behavior. When we engage in a new behavior, we create a new network and synaptic firing system that supports it, and every time we carry out that behavior the network fires and reinforces the behavior, which in turn strengthens the network.

Simply put, the more a sequence of neurons fires, the more prominent its network becomes and the quicker its sequence will fire, causing that behavior to be carried out sooner and with more frequency. This not only ensures that it will be more likely for us to repeat that behavior in the future but even more difficult *not* to.

Amazingly, over twenty-five hundred years ago, the Buddha understood this and said,

> *We are what we think.*
> *All that we are arises with our thoughts.*
> *What we think we become.*
> *With our thoughts we make the world.*

And because of understanding this, he warned, "Your worst enemy cannot harm you as much as your own unguarded thoughts."

When the modern science of neuroplasticity is put into Buddhist terms, it explains how our conditioning is ingrained and our reactivity becomes habitual. In understanding this process, the Buddha taught that both harmful and helpful mindsets are temporary experiences, based on temporary conditions.

As a result, he directs us in the *fourth tactical application of effort*: to sustain new helpful mindsets.

The Buddha understood that we need to sustain wholesome and helpful mindsets to escape from being held hostage by our old thinking and its reactive ways. And that to sustain these new wholesome mindsets requires the continuous firing of their neuronal sequences, not only to strengthen the network and make it easier for us to maintain positive mindsets but for this neurological sequence to fire when we need it to— not only from being triggered by circumstances outside ourselves but through our own intentions and efforts.

What this means is that a neuronal network sequence can be fired simply as a result of our applying our intention and effort to do so. The Buddha discovered that while in the midst of an unwholesome mindset, we can use our effort to simultaneously create a wholesome mindset, and in doing so shift our attention to it. This was a radical insight for his time, as it detailed the breaking of attachment and the changing of our mind exactly as modern day science does.

Since "changing our mind" is vitally important, the next tactics of the plan are training ourselves in the mental discipline required to create and sustain this effort: *Wise Mindfulness and Wise Concentration.*

WISE MINDFULNESS

Mindfulness is the ability to be present with what is happening in the present. It is the ability to sustain one's bare attention on a general field of awareness. The purpose of mindfulness is to deconstruct experience to its foundational conditions. To see the difference between reality and our idea of reality (**change**), to understand that all conditioned experience is impermanent and ultimately an experience of dissatisfaction (**pain**), and to experience that there is "no self" to be found (**conditionality**).

Utilizing mindfulness, we deconstruct experience to its most basic conditioned level so that we will be able to see that things exist differently from the way we *think* they do. When we clearly see the different aspects that must come together to create experience, and that they are constantly shifting and changing, we change our tunnel-vision perception of things being fixed and permanent to a spacious and open view of how things constantly ebb and flow.

This wisdom then leads us to the *first purpose of mindfulness*: to see the difference between reality and our idea of it. This wisdom is twofold. First, when we can clearly see that things are never exactly as we wish them to be we can become more relaxed and flexible with our expectations. This enables us to not only accept them but to find satisfaction in them. And second, when things are legitimately bad we can see that they are not nearly as bad as we think they are. This enables us to break attachment to our desire and aversion and be with things as they are, without trying to prematurely end them or abnormally prolong them.

The *second purpose of mindfulness* is to observe that conditioned experience is ultimately dissatisfying. This insight teaches us that experience is impermanent because it is based on temporary conditions that will change, and that even when we are happy with the way things are, because the conditions that the situation is based upon will change and the experience will end, even happiness will ultimately cause us pain.

In fact, we often sabotage things when they *are* good because we intrinsically know this. It immediately has an adverse effect on the experience, as just our wish for something not to end while we are in the midst of enjoying it is not only enough to dampen the experience but begins our descent into suffering.

An old Zen teaching says: "The way is not hard for those without preference and judgment, for those who do not pick and choose."

Now, this teaching is a little misleading, as it does not mean that we cannot have preferences and judgments, or pick and choose things based on them; it simply points to not being *attached* to them, flexible in our expectations, and able to adapt and redirect our focus when those expectations cannot be met.

The *third purpose of mindfulness* is to see that no permanent self exists in conditioned experience. As I touched upon in the discussion on emptiness, this is not saying that we do not exist, but rather, that we exist differently from the way we think we do.

The teaching is not that the self does not exist but that it, too, is made up of temporary conditions that are not inherent to it. Rather than this being a philosophical issue or a metaphysical experience, this is a practical, skillful way to relate to ourselves and free ourselves from suffering by dismantling its causes, which are rooted in our harmful conditioned beliefs, thinking, and habitual reactions.

To respond skillfully to these insights, we must utilize the *fourth tactical application of wise effort*: **concentration.**

Concentration is an acute focus on objects and activity within the general field of awareness. It is a tool we use within mindfulness to slow down our perception to a static point and hold our awareness steady on the object or activity that mindfulness has made us present for.

The teachings describe that there are four foundations of mindfulness, and that each one has a designated concentration.

The *first designated concentration of mindfulness* is **form.** This refers to our awareness of our physical experience. Like a bodyguard doing surveillance of all the perimeter entrypoints and the interior checkpoints of the compound they are tasked with securing, we bring our focus to the body's "sense doors"—the entrypoints to our inner Buddha's compound that we are tasked with securing.

As I discussed earlier, the sense doors are our points of contact with the material world and are identified as the eyes, ears, nose, tongue, body, and mind. In this instance, we concentrate on their process rather than their content, as *we see without looking, hear without listening, smell and taste without savoring or repulsion, touch without discrimination,* and *have thoughts without thinking.* This simply means that we are aware that we are seeing, hearing, smelling, tasting, touching, and thinking without adding a narrative that sweeps us away from the awareness of the physical experience.

Just as the bodyguard monitors the activity at the checkpoints along the perimeter of the compound they are securing, and investigates breaches before making a final assessment, likewise, as we act as our inner Buddha's bodyguard, we must inspect the activity of our inner checkpoints before we make any determination on how to respond.

We do this by experiencing the sensations of the body, such as heat, coolness, tightness, looseness, itching, pulsing, throbbing, and so on. We do this without adding a mistaken mental evaluation of it and making a faulty assessment, which in turn leads us to create an incident where there would have been none.

So how do we make an accurate assessment? We must identify the temporary conditions that create the physical experience, and observe how the experience is impermanent. Observing the impermanence of the experience keeps us from hastily responding and making it worse. In this case, staying in the experience of the sensations keeps us from jumping to an assessment of it being either pleasant or unpleasant. This keeps us from being swept toward mental suffering by the narrative that comes with such an assessment.

Here is an example that might seem a bit extreme, but I think it illustrates the point perfectly. As a martial artist and defensive tactics instructor, I teach people how to protect themselves from a knife attack, and the first thing I tell them is that they should expect to get cut, and that if, Buddha forbid, they get stabbed, to not pull the knife out. Leaving the knife in will at least keep the wound closed and lessen the blood loss, as it will clot on the blade; hastily pulling the knife out would open the wound and accelerate blood loss, with immediate, detrimental consequences.

A comparable example of this in Buddhist practice would be when we are sitting in meditation and suddenly feel a sharp pain in our back or knees. Usually, the moment we are "stabbed" with pain during meditation, we react like a person "pulling the knife out": without thinking, we hastily move and shift our position to relieve the pain. Even though it seems to work, what we don't realize is that we've expedited the "bleeding." The relief is only temporary, and moments later, we find ourselves experiencing new pain and moving again, then moments later we experience new pain, which in turn makes us move yet again. This happens over and over until, as with bleeding, we are in a constant flow of motion rather than sitting still.

Just as a bodyguard orders the victim to leave the knife in, the meditation teacher orders us not to move, to stay present with the experience as it is, and observe it exactly for what it is—simply a tight, hot, throbbing phenomenon. As we stay with the experience, we clearly observe how it is the result of temporary conditions and, as those conditions change, so will our experience of the phenomenon we label pain.

The issue of naming or labeling the sensations of the experience is important in this process. When we experience the sensations of what we ultimately call pain, such as tightness, throbbing, burning, and so on, we should not label it as pain, as to do so would cause us to get swept away in adding a narrative about the experience.

What we do is acknowledge the experience by labeling the sensations for exactly what they are. As we experience sensations we note them and let them pass, just as we would with random thoughts. If we feel tightness, we simply note to ourselves "tightness"; if we are feeling a burning sensation, we simply note to ourselves "burning"; and so on.

We engage the experience by observing the ways in which the conditions that give rise to the tightness or burning are shifting and changing. As we experience the shifting subtleties and nuances of the sensations, we see how they directly correlate with the degree to which we feel them, until we suddenly realize that not only has the pain dissipated and left but that it was exacerbated by our thinking about it. There is no need for us to identify with it.

Now, I'm not saying that we should sit in pain and injure ourselves; just that we should sit long enough to begin to have this learning experience, then use it as a catalyst to sit longer and longer each time. In other words, leave the damned knife in!

The designated concentration for the *second foundation of mindfulness* is **feeling,** which deals with the effect that the contact we made in the first foundation is having on us. The effect of the contact we made is identified by three categorizations: **pleasant, unpleasant,** or **neutral.**

The first aspect of mindfulness of feeling is simply to know that we are feeling what we are feeling. When we do so, we are not dealing with the emotional content but simply, the general experiential tone of the contact.

Just as we did when experiencing contact with the form, we note the experience. So, if the experience is unpleasant, we simply acknowledge the unpleasant feeling without adding a narrative about it or trying to change it. As we do this, we experience the impermanence of our feelings. We see how, due to temporary conditions, feelings change by themselves, as from moment to moment what is extremely unpleasant can shift to being mildly unpleasant, and what's mildly pleasant can become extremely pleasant. We see the harm in completely identifying with our experience, and the value in dealing with it as a temporary occurrence.

The first and second foundations of mindfulness are practices of describing the texture of our experience. They broaden our field of awareness so that we see the continually changing conditions that shift our experience—from unpleasant to pleasant, pleasant to unpleasant, and neutral to either pleasant or unpleasant.

The *third foundation of mindfulness* is **evaluation** of the feeling experience. This does not mean we think about it or add a narrative, but simply investigate and label or note what we have evaluated.

The next *designated concentration of mindfulness* is of the **mental state** that has arisen due to our contact and resulting feeling experience. This concentration has three categorizations: **suffering**, **bliss**, and **equanimity**.

In this foundation, we investigate our desire and aversion in relation to these states via the subcategories of their conditions, such as greed, hate, loving-kindness, and compassion. As with mindfulness of feelings, when mindful of mental states, we are investigating the quality of each state itself, as well as the temporary conditions that cause each state to shift from one to another. In both the second and third foundations of mindfulness, we begin to identify our habitual patterns, which are the foundation of our working with attachment.

While the third foundation of mindfulness evaluates the quality of the mental state, the fourth foundation of mindfulness acutely explores the dynamics at work within that mental state, so the *designated concentration for the fourth foundation of mindfulness* is **Mental Phenomenon**. This is categorized as an investigation of how the phenomenon works and how we can work with it, whether it be in weakening harmful conditioning or in strengthening helpful conditioning.

As we explore the workings of our mental experience, the teachings of the hindrances, the sense doors, the five conditions, the four noble truths, and all other mental events become the objects of our investigation. Our investigation is not only of their presence, or lack thereof, but of their functioning and our interaction with them. We are not merely observing, as in the previous foundation practices; we are either skillfully engaging and cultivating them or abandoning them.

While it's urgent that we apply the tactics of mindfulness and concentration with laserlike precision to our thoughts, conduct, and speech, a subtler and perhaps more important application is to use them in order to be aware of the fact that we are *not* using them.

Simply put, we must consistently use these tactics in order to remind ourselves to use them. By applying the tactics of mindfulness and concentration, we are able to be mindful and concentrated and this will consistently remind us of the practice we must do and ensure that we are vigilant in doing it.

So, now that I've briefed you on the basic boot camp training and tactics of becoming a bodyguard of the Buddha, let me brief you on the special forces that are called in when a more elite strike force is needed to protect our notorious VIP from his greatest threats.

8

The Buddha's Special Forces

We've all heard the motivational statement "practice makes perfect," but Buddhist teaching says that "practice *is* perfection," that meditation does not *lead* to enlightenment but that the act of meditation itself *is* enlightenment.

Our inner Buddha, the notorious VIP we are protecting, is actually the manifestation of this innate quality of perfection that already exists in each one of us.

This perfection manifests in what's called *bodhicitta*, which is defined as having the wish or desire to attain enlightenment for oneself and others. Bodhicitta (pronounced bodie-cheetah) spontaneously rises when we break our attachment to the illusion of a permanent self that is rooted in attachment to the fixed constructs that cause a dualistic view. *Bodhi* is translated as "awakened" and *citta* as "mind." While to have bodhicitta (or as I prefer to call it "awakened mind") might seem like a lofty "spiritual" attainment, it's actually grounded in compassion for the reality of the human experience.

The practitioner who has experienced bodhicitta, who has the aspirations that stem from it, and who engages in the actions to carry out those bodhicitta aspirations is called a *bodhisattva*. A bodhisattva, rather than being focused on just their own personal life, is focused on the whole of humanity and is willing to do whatever it takes to save it, to sacrifice themselves for the good of all.

I liken this transformation to going from an enlisted man who has completed boot camp and is a foot soldier in the Buddha's revolutionary army to entering an elite level of training and joining the Buddha's special forces. So, next, I'll brief you on the special mission of these elite special forces operatives.

To be a bodhisattva, a team member of the Buddha's elite special forces, not only means that one agrees to take on a higher level of mission but that one is able to achieve the mission objective due to their development of a higher level of tactical ability.

As I mentioned earlier, the teachings describe this higher level of tactical ability as the innate qualities of perfection, and breaks them into six directives of practice, while further identifying these directives as being the qualities of enlightenment. (There are actually Ten Perfections taught, but I've stuck to the first six, as they tend to be the same in all traditions, while the last four tend to differ among different traditions.)

As I mentioned earlier when I discussed the basic proactive tactical applications in the context of our conduct within the Buddha's Eight-fold Tactical Plan, these Six Directives of Practice, or **Perfections**, are a more elite level of operation and are defined as: **Generosity**, **Morality**, **Patience**, **Energy**, **Meditation**, and **Wisdom**. (Like most Buddhist teachings the practice of the Six Perfections has a linear and all-encompassing trajectory, and while my briefing you of these tactics will be a linear one, it's important to note not only their interconnectedness but that there is a nearly simultaneous experience of them during practice.)

At its most obvious, generosity is the giving of material things in support of the most fundamental survival needs. Food, shelter, clothes, household items, and monetary donations are all ways that many people contribute. While this type of giving is vitally important, the teachings also speak of a different type of generosity: giving of oneself.

This deeper level of teaching starts by pointing out that what's most important about the giving of material things is not the item but the act of giving itself, as the act of giving is dependent on our mindset.

To be a bodhisattva, we must cultivate a state of mind of giving freely without hesitation or regret. It is also imperative that our intention in giving is free of any desire for recognition or acclaim; if it isn't, rather than *giving* we are actually *taking*.

Giving in this manner becomes easier through repetition and becomes a transformative experience unto itself, as we go from a point where we had to work with our resistance in order to give to being able to find satisfaction just in the act of giving. This satisfaction begins by cultivating the ability to let go of material things, which is the gateway we must go through to cultivate the depth of giving of the self at the heart of this teaching.

Once we have reached the point of being an "elite" practitioner doing an "elite" practice, at first glance, it might seem that giving would be easier rather than harder. But this assumption is the result of mistaken thinking, wherein we think that since we are not giving anything material, or of "value," we have nothing we need to work at relinquishing.

What we quickly learn is that giving of the self is actually the hardest thing to give, as it is the most valuable thing we have *to* give. What we had thought was giving *nothing* turns out to be giving *everything*, as rather than just being able to hand off an item or money and turn away from the situation, giving of the self requires us to relinquish our resistance to turning toward the situation, to engaging it with openness, vulnerability, and patience, as we persevere to its conclusion.

To give of the self means that we must engage the experience *with* the person. We must see what they see and feel what they feel. It requires us to make a commitment to be there for them and to *not* be there for ourselves, which often is even harder for us to do, as it requires a selflessness that is rooted in rigorous empathy and compassion.

This seems like it would be easy for a dedicated Buddhist, but many practitioners find the shift from the self-cherishing type experience that led them to seek transformation in the first place to a focus exclusively on caring for another's plight is extremely difficult, especially when they perceive that doing so is taking them out of enjoying the "self-help" benefits they have begun to experience from their own practice. The irony is that rather than eroding the "self-help" benefit of their practice, it strengthens it and fosters an even greater transformation, which in turn results in an even greater "self-help" benefit.

This greater transformation of generosity, while it is rooted in developing the ability to give material items, cultivates empathy and compassion and the development of the quality of selflessness and leads to developing the desire to help others on a much deeper level.

Rather than being focused on just their immediate survival needs (this does not diminish the importance of attending to their survival needs, as stabilizing their immediate material problems is what creates the opportunity to focus on deeper problems), or on the giving of ourselves in terms of the time we offer, we turn our focus to their suffering and deepen our generosity with the giving of an unconditional emotional support, which culminates in the generosity of the giving of the dharma.

This is not our attempt to convert the person to Buddhism, but a sharing of wisdom, personal insight, and the experience of our practical application of the teachings we've used to contend with our own pain. In doing so, we share the skillfulness of how we have utilized the dharma ourselves and teach others how they can use it as well in response to their own painful circumstances.

Up to this point our practice has been about *taking* refuge, but now through this generosity practice we learn how to *give* refuge. Just as a suffering person's survival needs must be dealt with first, before our deeper emotional issues are dealt with, taking refuge is, at first, tending to our own emotional survival needs. And while vitally important, as it is the necessary stabilization that we need to be able to progress to a deeper level of practice, in the big picture it is not enough.

The deeper transformation the teachings urge us to find in our generosity practice is to bring refuge to all beings. This involves committing to working toward protecting all living beings, meaning that everything we do is rooted in taking action for the betterment of all. This can range from being active in anti-war work; the preserving of civil rights, animal rights, and ecological concerns; to becoming vegetarian or vegan; to saving that spider from going down your shower drain. It's about doing what's needed to protect all beings. We cannot turn away; we must do *everything* we can.

Taking this practice even deeper, we move from protecting all beings to bringing happiness to all beings. This is more than just having the desire to do so. This is about reaching a depth in our practice of being willing to love unconditionally, even our enemies. This ability is the greatest depth of generosity, and in my experience, the hardest part of the teaching. It takes a long time and a lot of hard work, to be so selfless and benevolent.

The meditative teaching of *metta* (lovingkindness) directs us to cultivate this unconditional love and kindness in a specific order that begins first applying it to **ourselves**, then to a **benefactor**, a **friend**, a **neutral** person, a **difficult** person, and finally **all beings**.

Personally, I had (and still have) a hard time with this. It's important to follow this progression from the easiest person (usually ourselves, but I do understand that for some this could be the hardest stage) to the hardest person (all beings, especially our enemies!), with each stage making the next one easier. But in full disclosure, there have been many times in my practice when I have worked painstakingly hard at this, and even though I was able to reach the point where I could "love my enemy," a new one would attack and I had to go right back to the beginning of the process to be able to reach that same point with my new nemesis.

So don't always expect to be able to maintain operation lovingkindness without constant maintenance and upgrades.

While in my experience, this process has gotten easier (even if "getting easier" was a miniscule amount each time), its getting easier has come not only due to the end benefit that results from doing it but from the self-transformation that comes as a result of engaging in *doing it*, regardless of the end results.

What the process deeply affects is what is at the root of our intention, as our transformation is one of weakening our conditioning and challenging our harmful, long-held fixed ideas and beliefs. This transformation into selflessness via the practice of generosity changes us at our core. It redefines our ethics and reveals our virtues, as it grounds us in a new morality. (The transformation that results from metta practice directly ties in to our karma, which I will address in depth later.)

As I mentioned earlier, the result of renunciation practice and the purpose of making conduct commitments is to weaken our harmful conditioning and create new, helpful conditioning that helps us develop new ethical behavior. In the practice of the Six Perfections, those new ethics are the foundation of our new morality. Though morality and ethics might often be viewed as the same thing, and perhaps distinguishing a difference could be considered semantics, in my experience I think it's an important, necessary distinction.

In this context, ethics would refer to a general description or code of behavior that Buddhists more or less agree upon as a group, while morals would refer to the character of the individual *within* the group, making morality the ability to be disciplined in the application of ethics.

This difference points to how, as new Buddhists, we take on certain ethical practices because we are told to by Buddhism or because a teacher has urged us to, rather than because *we* have any conviction in them ourselves. But this is our starting point, as the work we do that stems from being told to do it is the work that transforms us on a deeper level, which enables us to develop a personal moral code of action.

Simply put, rather than needing to be told what to do, much like a behavioral modification directive, the behavior becomes an organic extension of our intrinsic wisdom. Rather than "acting as if," we transcend the need to act at all and are able to spontaneously do the right thing, to do what's skillful and appropriate without having to process a set of mandated directives as guidance.

This natural ability to appropriately respond creates a new demeanor of composure, which the teachings define as **patience**. In this context, patience is defined as the ability to endure. The teachings define this endurance as the ability to endure the hardship caused by others, of our own suffering, and of the truth. That truth is how our attachment to our self-cherishing is at the root of all our unhappiness, and on a deeper level, it is discovering that this self we're attached to does not exist at all. It is the truth of the nature of existence and its inherent dissatisfaction.

When it comes to enduring the hardships caused by others, there are definitely conflicts we must face whose causes are rooted in dynamics outside ourselves (whether purposely done toward us with malice, or we are innocently hit by "friendly" fire from those with whom we have relationships, or we are truly the victim of a completely random act), but ultimately, it remains our responsibility to own our reaction and our response. This aspect of endurance is perfecting the ability to not immediately engage in blame and seek retribution, but to cultivate understanding and compassion, particularly toward ourselves. In cultivating this ability, we learn to not turn our pain into suffering.

But don't mistake this endurance as a type of "suffering through" things. Remember, we are talking about the practice of the "perfections," meaning that this is our practice at its best, that this is *us* at *our* best.

So this endurance refers to us going through hardship in the most appropriate, constructive, skillful way possible. Not only are we *not* attached, pursuing, or avoiding but attachment, pursuit, or avoidance were never options in the first place when faced with the adversity.

There's a big difference between our first rudimentary understanding of the Four Noble Truths and the nature of suffering and our later understanding of it as it pertains to the Perfection of Endurance practice. Now, rather than seeing hardship as something we take personally and must combat, we take it in stride as just a normal part of living, as something to be expected that we can comfortably manage. Now, rather than hardship causing a fight-or-flight reaction that puts us in a desperate survival mode, we find that we do not feel threatened, nor do we feel that all we can do is muster the ability to survive. On the contrary, we find that we can thrive, and that this thriving energizes us.

This leads us to the next perfection, which is the energy that results from endurance.

With my background in martial arts, I really love the traditional Buddhist way of defining energy, which uses the metaphors of donning armor and carrying out heroic behavior characterized by the courage and fearlessness used by a warrior to defeat his enemies. But it's actually much simpler than that.

As one of the hindrances (or as I prefer to call them, "threats"), sleepiness means more than just being physically tired; it is defined as laziness in not doing the things in our practice that we need to do. The perfection of energy now deepens to include discovering a new-found energy and a *proactive* diligence and enthusiasm *to* do our practice.

This diligence and enthusiasm is at the foundation of the next perfection, which is **meditation**.

The classical definition of the perfection of meditation uses words like *concentration, mindfulness,* and *contemplation* to describe the process of how to perfect meditation. My interpretation, however, is that it should be called *mental discipline,* "the training of the mind."

Traditional Buddhists would say that this training of the mind's purpose is to achieve enlightenment, but my view is that the result of this mental discipline should be to clearly see reality and respond wisely.

I view this perfection not as something we achieve but as something we *do*, and as we focus our mind on *doing* the tasks of Buddhism, we deepen our realization. This deeper realization is not of lofty, supernatural truths but the wisdom that comes from being better able to clearly see the truth of the reality directly in front of us.

So, the next perfection is the **wisdom** that results from our mental discipline. This is not to say that wisdom is knowledge. Wisdom is not information we learn; rather, it is the discovery of our own intuitive, intrinsic understanding, which is revealed during our direct experience.

When we first start learning the teachings of Buddhism, it is on an intellectual level. Because of this, our first practice efforts are rooted in *thinking* about Buddhism rather than in *doing* Buddhism. While this thinking might be beneficial at times, we must realize that insight is not merely the result of an absence of ignorance.

Ignorance is deceptively two pronged: not only can it precede wisdom and unknowingly put us on a path *away* from insight but it can also be the result of our thinking about our knowledge and coming to a wrong view based upon it, which we mistake for valid insight.

This dilemma will happen from time to time, no matter how hard we are practicing. Sometimes, it will misdirect and delay us on our journey. However, it is a natural, and I would say, sometimes needed occurrence on the path, as we learn to work through illusion and delusion and assimilate the teachings and put them into action.

A traditional Buddhist teaching speaks of how the greatest insights can come from when we are within the deepest delusion. It uses the image of the lotus flower blooming from the mud as a metaphor to convey this. Lotus flowers are found growing in dark, murky, muddy waters, yet in spite of this seemingly impossible adversity, they miraculously rise and bloom. Some say in spite of it, but I say *because* of it.

The Buddha said: "Those who are deluded about realization are sentient beings. Those who have great realization about delusion are Buddhas."

What the Buddha was pointing out is that the most insidious aspect of delusion is that the person does not realize that they are deluded. It is an inability to clearly see the truth that makes a person misunderstand their experience and *think* they have experienced enlightenment, and is what keeps them from experiencing enlightenment. The ability to recognize delusion is only possible *due* to enlightenment.

We experience realizations on many levels and from different perspectives, but the general realization the teachings direct us toward comes as a result of experiencing *emptiness.*

Earlier, I touched on emptiness as it relates to our understanding of the self; now we will discuss perfecting this understanding and its application by addressing emptiness as it relates to the self and as the self relates to others.

We have already discovered that there is nothing inherent in any conditioned experience, nothing fixed and permanent to grasp, nothing with its own separate existence, and that everything that exists is dependent on other conditions. Now, we deepen our practice and begin to practice experiencing this emptiness via situational interactions with others—the real-life way to practice this and all the other perfections I've discussed in this section. The teachings say that practice *is* perfection, but we all have had enough experience to know that practice does not make us perfect.

On the contrary, what this teaching is referring to is that we realize the innate goodness within each of us and welcome the opportunity to see it in others and reveal it within ourselves.

Is it really possible? Well, that "interdepends" … on how well we abide by and enforce the law of karma.

9

The Operational Theater
of Karma

*K*arma is one of those Buddhist words that has become prevalent (and misunderstood and misused) in our culture, so I think it's important to define the term as I understand it and apply it, before briefing you on how a bodhisattva tactically applies it.

Just as the bodyguard does not believe that the outcome of a protection detail is the result of fate or destiny (either due to conditions beyond the control of an agent or team or the unavoidable consequence of the team's actions or inaction), I do not believe the Buddhist law of karma to be a governing factor that results in a metaphysically decided, unavoidable consequence of fate in life.

I think it's very important to stress several points before we go further: First, my definition of the word "law" in this context and, second, my classification of karma as having two distinct parts.

The standard definition of "law" describes a set of rules a majority consensus has mandated to regulate specific actions one chooses to follow to avoid receiving a penalty. In a Buddhist context, though, I am defining "law" to mean a statement of irrefutable fact drawn from observation and experience that describes the relational dynamic between cause and effect. As a law, karma is not a directive that we are able to choose to be affected by or not; it is a governing dynamic that will occur, regardless of our choosing to recognize its effect in our lives or not.

With this understanding in mind, my first classification of karma is what I call to *abide by the law of karma* and the second classification is to *enforce the law of karma*.

Abide by the Law of Karma

To abide by the law of karma is to acknowledge and accept it as the governing dynamic in how all interacting conditions work.

When we abide, we understand that while all cause and effect has the potential to impact us in some way, that impact does not have to be internalized as being personal. This means that the results from the myriad causes and effects that are constantly playing out around us are not intentionally directed at us, nor do they require anything more from us than to acknowledge them and *not* make them personal.

I know this might seem to contradict even what I have said about karma, but it doesn't. What I am addressing here is exactly what I discussed earlier in regard to the perfection of patience, and how we must endure "friendly fire."

The fact is that our lives are often filled with uncomfortable situations, unforeseen dilemmas, and potential conflicts that arise out of neutral circumstances, as well as from other people's actions. There is no need to own it as our "bad" karma resulting from our own "bad" karma. This doesn't mean that we do not address these situations; it simply means that we don't assign a deeper personal meaning to them as the reason that they occur.

This first classification of karma, of abiding, happens within the parameters of what I call the **Operational Theater of Karma**. In military terms, "theater" refers to any area that can be invaded and defended, as it becomes the backdrop in which a conflict takes place.

In a Buddhist context, I am using the word "theater" to denote the conditions of pain, change, and impermanence, and the inherent dissatisfaction, trials, and tribulations that will *always* invade and threaten us. These conditions will always be the backdrop that we will find ourselves operating within, in spite of our intentions and actions. To *abide* by the law of karma is to *accept* this inevitability.

As Dogen poetically said: "Flowers will die even as we cherish their bloom, and weeds will grow even as we wish them to die."

I have always felt released and freed not shackled or imprisoned in my experience of abiding by the law of karma, but what I've found within the Buddhist community is a drastically different understanding of what I am calling the Operational Theater of Karma.

What I've found is that most practitioners experience the result of the law of karma as feeling like they have been judged, convicted, sentenced, and incarcerated by a "hanging judge" deity who is judging their worth as a person, and they can be acquitted of their heinous karmic crime only if they commit a sort of "jury tampering" by using "merit" as a way to bribe the powers that be and get off!

The end result of this understanding of karma is that it plays out much like a "sin and redemption" dynamic, as the person ends up being filled with either self-righteous arrogance or self-loathing shame.

For me, what really makes this understanding miss the mark is why these practitioners believe this view of karma. Their belief is vested in the perspective that a higher power (deities, a god, the universe, and so forth) is making a decision to punish or reward them based on the type of person they are judged to be, rather than the inevitable outcome of their actions.

This understanding of the law of karma points to a deeper issue, which is rooted in the self-judgment and shame many people carry that is derived from their harmful conditioning and long-standing suffering over painful, even traumatic experiences from which they have not yet healed (more on this later).

Before you get offended, thinking that I'm being critical of Judeo-Christian beliefs, let me say that it might surprise you to know that I'm not just talking about Western converts. This is true, if not more so, of those coming from a strictly traditional Buddhist indoctrination in the East, as they too have a very similar understanding of karma. Most traditional Buddhist cultures teach that same view. This is not because Eastern practitioners and their cultures misunderstand karma, but rather because this same view, or better yet *belief*, is simply what they have been taught, believe, and continue to teach, and what the first teachers taught when they came to the West.

Again, it's not my intention to be critical, but before I further address my personal understanding and practical application of the law of karma, it is important to take a deeper look at the understanding found in the traditional Buddhist religion, because it is surprisingly similar to the Judeo-Christian view.

THE TRADITIONAL BUDDHIST VIEW OF KARMA

Like most religions, Buddhism has a faction that takes a literal view and a faction that takes a figurative view. But before we get into that discussion, I must first address the word "religion," as it has so many different meanings for people and baggage that seems to come along with it.

I define *being religious* as having the aspiration to reconcile one's deeper questions about the nature of existence and the meaning of one's life, and I define *religion* as the methodology one uses in the pursuit of fulfilling that aspiration. While this definition does apply to both the figurative and literal factions, what differs between the two groups is its strategic execution.

The strategic execution by *literal factions* is one that is dogmatic and rooted in the metaphysical teachings of accumulating merit for the purpose of securing a better future. It specifically entails purifying all bad karma and attaining complete liberation from *samsara* (a traditional word used to describe the repetitive circular cycle of suffering), to be born into a better existence in another lifetime.

The strategic execution by *figurative factions* is one that is pragmatic. It is rooted in the psychological understanding of the teachings as metaphors that guide practitioners to discern for themselves how to apply Buddhist teachings in a manner relative to liberation in the present moment, that is, liberation is achieved by ending the circular cycle of harmful habitual conditioning and reactivity and achieving a better existence in the next moment.

It is in this context that many Buddhists get confused, as they hear the literal Buddhists speak of *reincarnation* and the figurative Buddhists speak of *rebirth*. And while these two words are often used interchangeably by both factions, no matter which word they use, the literal Buddhist is always referring to their belief in going from one lifetime to another lifetime, while the figurative Buddhist is always referring to their understanding of going from moment to moment in this one and only lifetime.

This is not just semantics; it raises an important issue. In spite of all the Buddhist talk about engaging the present moment, the traditional teachings of karma in regard to the present moment focus *not* on the future as the very *next* moment, or even in *this* lifetime, but on future results in completely *different* realms and lifetimes!

This is a point of contention for me, as well as the literal and figurative factions, because when one's work with karma is focused only on its impact from one lifetime to the next rather than the effect the actions taken have in the present moment, not only might those actions be inappropriate for that moment but extremely harmful to it.

Here is an old story about this type of thinking.

> When Bodhidharma arrived in China from India and went before the
> emperor, the following dialogue took place:
>
> "I have built temples and ordained monks," Emperor Wu said to
> Bodhidharma. "What is my merit?"
>
> To which Bodhidharma replied, "No merit."
>
> Shocked at being told this, the emperor then asked, "Then what is the
> first principle of the holy teachings?"
>
> "Vast emptiness, nothing holy," replied Bodhidharma.

In general, we suffer when our intention is not pure but rooted in what
we hope to gain, either in the next moment or the next lifetime. And
when we start deciding what is holy and what is not we also suffer,
because we get caught up in the separation created by our attachment
to such ideas.

This highlights the difference between a metaphysical and psychological understanding, as the literal Buddhist believes that their actions are
a way of gaining merit *with*, and in turn favor *from*, an outside force
that will determine the quality of their reincarnation, while the figurative Buddhist engages in their actions as an exercise in reinforcing that
particular action and ingraining a future resolve to continually engage
in it (here is the connection between neuroplasticity and karma that
I promised earlier), which results in a rebirth or entry into the next
moment with an improvement in circumstances that they understand as
the hard-earned result of their own determination and footwork.

The figurative Buddhist recognizes that rather than being saved
by an outside power, their future rests on them saving themselves by
cultivating the ability to take responsibility for it by abandoning harmful
actions and engaging in wholesome ones.

My experience in doing this, in understanding karma and best working with it, is to see it as nothing more than cause, effect, and the actions that we take in response. And while we can say that when one does "good" things that good things will result, and when one does "bad" things that bad things will result, it's vital to understand that this does not hinge on a moral or ethical assessment of whether or not we are a "good" or "bad" person, for as the law dictates, a good act will have a good result and a bad act will have a bad result regardless of who is doing the deed.

While on an intellectual level we might accept this, the problem that most of us have with working with it, is how we subjectively define what is "good" and "bad," and more importantly, if whether we are honestly investigating the intention behind the acts that we are subjectively assessing as either "good" or "bad."

Another aspect of difficulty we have in working with this understanding is that we will often blame ourselves for causing our own difficulties. This is different from taking responsibility for one's ill intent and owning the harmful actions that arise from it. Practitioners who view themselves as "bad" will automatically attribute something bad in their life (even when it cannot be attributed to any particular action of theirs) as the result of their having "bad karma," as though it were a curse arising from their innate "badness."

Ironically, this conviction that one is "cursed with bad karma" directly contradicts the teaching of the First Noble Truth in Buddhism. As I discussed earlier, in addressing the First Noble Truth and ambush scenarios, the nature of our existence is one of dissatisfaction. At times, we all will face pain, loss, blame, and disrepute, regardless of our intentions or our actions.

While the teachings of the First Noble Truth and the ambush experiences might seem to contradict the teachings of karma they do not.

They support the perspective that karma is *not* a subjectively applied punishment doled out by a morally judgmental deity or universe. For one to think that it is extremely harmful and self-perpetuating. In the view of the person stuck in this vicious cycle, the results of that self-perpetuation then become the "proof" they use to validate their belief and stay stuck in it.

We will often have to face hardships in our lives that result from happenstance and the karmic actions of others rather than our own actions. Focusing on whether or not it is our "bad" karma that is the cause is not the most important issue, because the *why* of what we are experiencing doesn't necessarily direct us in *how* we need to best respond to create new karma for ourselves, moving forward.

The Buddha used a story about a man who has been shot by a poison arrow to address the issue of needing to know *why* things are occurring, and the peril associated with that *needing* to know. In the sutra, the story is used in a more general way to address the many deep, metaphysical questions practitioners have, but I feel it addresses the point of this discussion perfectly.

THE BUDDHA SAID:

It's just as if a man were wounded by a poisoned arrow. When his family and friends provide him with a doctor the wounded man would say, "I will not have this arrow removed until I know if the man that wounded me is a noble warrior, a priest, a merchant, or a worker." The wounded man would say, "I won't have this arrow removed until I know the given name of the man that wounded me and the name of his clan... until I know if he is tall, of medium height, or short... until I know whether he is dark or golden colored... until I know his home village, town, or city... until I know whether the bow string that fired the arrow was made of fiber, bamboo, sinew, hemp, or bark... until I know if the arrow shaft with which I was wounded was wild or cultivated... until I know if the feathers on the arrow shaft with which I was wounded were from a vulture, stork, hawk, or peacock." He would say, "I won't have this arrow removed until I know if the arrow that I was wounded with was that of a common arrow, a curved arrow, a barbed, calf toothed, or an oleander arrow." This man would die and all those things would remain unknown to him.

The *why* I am addressing is not in the context of cause and effect (cause is obviously the *why* of the resulting effect) but in the context of the practitioner being caught in the trap of needing to define *why*, as well as having to make it personal, especially in attributing the *why* to their own "bad" karma and believing themselves to be a "bad" person.

While at times it is important and helpful to understand the *why* of our karma, it should not prevent us from addressing the threat we face with immediate countermeasures.

We see this in the protocol of how protection agents immediately respond to a threat. When two bodyguards are working a protective detail they walk in a designated formation around the client. While in formation, the agent in front of the client is called the "pointman" and the agent behind the client is considered the "evacuation agent." The pointman's job is to alert the evacuation agent to a threat. This is done verbally, with a short, quick, simple shout, as there is no time to waste.

As the pointman recognizes an attack and responds to it with physical intervention, he yells, "Threat!" If the pointman sees a weapon he would yell "Weapon!" And if the weapon can be identified, he would yell, "Gun" or "Knife!" If the threat comes from the rear, without a moment of hesitation the agents would switch roles and the evacuation agent would now take on the pointman's responsibilities and the pointman would be responsible for covering and evacuating the client.

The efficiency of a protection detail hinges upon agents not wasting a moment getting caught up in the *why* of things or what they know, don't know, or *think* they know about the attack, but in instantly carrying out their objective in spite of what they don't know.

So upon hearing just this one word, the evacuation agent springs into action and grabs the client around the waist from behind, bends them over, pushes their head down, and spins them around, shielding the bent-over client with their own body as they remove the client from the area. The agents' *only* concern is to respond appropriately to best protect their client. To carry out their objective they require no more information. In fact, any attempt to assess the situation beyond a first response would be extremely detrimental to its successful execution, as the success of an agent's initial response depends upon an immediate acceptance of the circumstance.

As you might have guessed by now, it is the figurative moment-to-moment perspective that I will address in my practical application of karma.

I'm aware that my phrasing of karma as something to *apply* might seem contradictory to my explanation of it being the governing directive of cause and effect. But as it pertains to ultimate truth (the Operational Theater of Karma), karma is just the law of cause and effect that simply states that for every action there will always be a reaction, while dealing with the relative (tactically applying karma), as it pertains to how we act and our intention behind the act.

The teachings tell us that it is our mission objective to sustain a wholesome mind, investigate and regulate our actions, and more importantly, the intentions behind them, and assign us the directive to subvert the results of our past harmful karma. But rather than karma simply being about our having an understanding of how cause and effect works, more importantly, it mandates the rules for engaging it.

This engagement is rooted in a code of ethical commitments that form the basis of the tactics we use in that engagement. It creates the foundation of the plan of action we must undertake to protect our inner Buddha. Tactical karma involves understanding what we must do within the Operational Theater of Karma, so we will next take a look at those mission plans.

10

Tactical Karma

My second classification of karma, the *enforcement of the law of karma*, is how we respond in general to the effects of all causes, how we act in regard to creating our own circumstances, and how we respond to the results of those circumstances.

If *abiding by the law of karma* is to accept the inevitability of cause and effect invading our lives in an impersonal, general way, then *enforcing the law of karma* involves identifying the actions we must take to defend our inner Buddha's life when it is personally threatened.

In this second part of the karma briefing, we will discuss the reactive and proactive tactics of what I call Tactical Karma. Again, tactical karma addresses how we enforce the law within the parameters of the Operational Theater of Karma. The operational theater is the stage for the mission, while the tactics are how we carry out that mission.

First Directive of Tactical Karma

There are two directives of tactical karma. The first is that we have the ability to change our mind.

Earlier, I briefed you on the Eight Tactics, specifically with regard to how we must apply effort. As a result of neuroplasticity, we can rewire our brain to think differently and have it direct us to *act* differently. The figurative Buddhist understands that it is their responsibility to abandon harmful actions and engage in wholesome ones, which dovetails with what we know about how neuroplasticity works, namely the practitioner's ability to disengage the firing of certain harmful neuronal sequences, while igniting wholesome ones.

For me, the process that neuroplasticity enables is not only the most sensible understanding of karma but the most realistic explanation of how to assimilate that understanding into applicable tactics in my life. While a literal Buddhist might be critical and dismissive because they see it as science and not relevant to their religion, my argument is that, as a result of experimenting with his own mind, the Buddha's teachings expounded on the same scientific theory.

In keeping with the bodyguard theme of this book, let's take a look at how neuroplasticity works by using a bomb as a metaphor for our ingrained, harmful conditioning, and that bomb exploding as a metaphor for acting out that harmful conditioning as our karma. As an example of tactical use of neuroplasticity, I will use the scenario of discovering the explosive device that has been planted and calling in the bomb squad as a metaphor for how to deal with the explosive situations that threaten to trigger us to act out our harmful, conditioned reactivity and how to diffuse them.

Just as a bomb is harmless without a detonator, and that detonation only comes from the wiring to the bomb being ignited by a trigger, we can also understand that our harmful conditioning is only harmful *if* it is triggered. Like a bomb squad, we must constantly patrol the minefield of our harmful thoughts, always prepared and ready to diffuse the ignition of the firing sequence that is wired to our harmful neuronal networks.

This is imperative to our mission, as the longer a bomb remains dormant the weaker the connection to its trigger becomes; likewise, the longer a neuronal network goes without being triggered and firing, the greater the chance it will not detonate.

Every time we are able to face a trigger and not act out our harmful reactivity, the repetitive habit of that behavior is weakened, making it more probable that the next time we face the same trigger, it will be easier for us to not react. The more this occurs the easier it will get, as it will take less effort to do so in the future.

This is the first stage of operation tactical karma. While keeping us safe, it is merely reactive, defensive tactics of restraint in response to old, harmful behavior. Although we are being skillful in its execution, it still is a constant operation of having to repeatedly diffuse our bombs, as we painstakingly try not to carelessly set them off, and if they do explode—and many times they will—the best we can do is to seek cover from the fallout.

This process of diffusing our mental bombs is nerve-racking, frustrating, tedious work. It requires extreme patience and diligence, as the explosive devices of our harmful conditioning have been so deeply embedded for so long, it often takes years of work to neutralize their threat.

So do not be surprised or dismayed, if as you diffuse your bombs in your practice, you feel like a desperate hero in a movie, with your back against the wall, your heart beating a mile a minute like it is about to burst out of your chest, your lungs heaving for air, sweat pouring into your eyes, as the timer frantically beeping down to zero rings loudly in your ears, and after you have done a tremendous amount of excruciatingly hard, painful work, you find that you were *just* lucky enough to pull the right wire out, *just* barely in the nick of time, *just* a mere moment before everything would have gone BOOM!

But isn't that how practice often goes for us? We stumble over a trip wire, set the detonation process in motion, and luckily, pull the right wire out of the bomb with barely a millisecond to spare! That's the insidiousness of the explosive devices that have been built from our past harmful, conditioned behavior. They are so deeply embedded within us that most of the time we're lucky if we are even able to take cover during their detonation, let alone diffuse them. But that doesn't mean Buddhist practice is always the doom and gloom of us ducking the shrapnel of our war-torn past.

Second Directive of Tactical Karma

This leads us to the second directive of operation tactical karma, which is about taking the initiative to be proactive in creating new, wholesome, helpful tactics that prevent the near enemies from planting any new explosive devices or triggering any detonations.

This is done by carrying out new, insightful, innovative methods of operation that secure our base from the enemy by not only strengthening our perimeter but also keep us from entering enemy territory and becoming vulnerable when we are out on patrol of our operational theater.

In Buddhist speak, this means that with new thinking and new actions we will not find ourselves in the old situations and relationships that can trigger us, and when we do, we can face those old triggers in a new skillful way and diffuse them.

As I have mentioned throughout the text, but specifically with reference to the conduct practices, being unclear about the intention behind an act makes assessing the result extremely difficult. This point is vital in the tactical application of karma, because often we will not see the immediate results of our actions; they must be assessed either over a short period of time, a long period of time, or sometimes cannot be assessed at all as we never experience the results.

As the saying goes, "Character is doing the right thing when no one is looking." So we must "do the right thing" regardless of whether we experience a benefit from it or not. Since we never know when, or even if, we will experience the results of our actions, we must have the courage of our convictions that the actions we take based on our intentions will result in our mission objective.

Another point to note is that because our actions often do not result in immediate helpful results, others can (and will) perceive our actions differently from how we intend them. This is not just because they have not been briefed on our mission objective, and therefore don't understand the intentions behind our actions, but the results they do observe and experience actually might be harmful to them, or at least they perceive them to be.

An example of this would be speaking the truth to a close friend with the intention of helping them come to terms with an issue. To the person being told the truth, who may not be ready to face it yet, as well as to a person witnessing the scenario, the action might be perceived as harmful, as it could be experienced as harsh and insulting speech, and the reaction of defensiveness and anger it triggers in the friend further supports the harmful perception. Often, it is only after time passes and the truth has been accepted (possibly having already fostered positive change in the person) that the intent behind the act can be understood and the result seen as helpful.

SUBJECTIVE CONDITIONS

While ultimately, over time, we do experience the results of most of our actions, the teachings note that those results are based upon the circumstances at the time of application, with the most prevalent being our quality of mind, the conviction behind our intentions, and the level of our commitment to the actions we take as a result.

These circumstances are identified as the **subjective conditions** and are defined as:

- **Persistent, repeated action**
- **Well-intentioned, determined action**
- **Regretless action**

The more determined we are to persist in the repetitive undertaking of applying our well-intentioned actions, and do so with no hesitation due to an ulterior motive, or with having expectations that if not met would cause us regret, the stronger the results of our actions will be. Here we have the Buddha's traditional directives of how to change our karma, which, with a modern perspective, is reminiscent of how to rewire our mind and change our conditioning via the strengthening of certain neuronal networks.

OBJECTIVE CONDITIONS

The other facet of determining the strength of our intentions and the actions that follow is identified as the **objective conditions**. These conditions are in relation to the person to whom our actions are directed at and are defined as:

- The quality of the recipient
- The relationship with the recipient

The traditional explanation of the "quality of the recipient" makes a distinction between castes or "classes" of recipients: *buddhas* (enlightened beings), *arhats* (beings that are worthy of enlightenment), and *lay people* (beings that are unworthy of enlightenment). My modern interpretation of the teachings identifies the different recipients more generally, as serious Buddhist practitioners, casual Buddhist practitioners, and non-practitioners.

The distinction between these classifications hinges on the depth of the recipients' Buddhist knowledge and their dedication to a spiritual pursuit rather than being qualified by their social position, as is traditional in Buddhism. The extent of the practitioner's willingness to engage those who are recipients of their helpful actions will directly correlate with the depth of their knowledge and understanding of spiritual pursuit and transformation.

Since the results of our tactical application of karma are partially dependent on the recipient, it makes sense that this dependence should be based not on the quality of the person as assessed by a moral judgment but on an assessment of their willingness to engage and how they engage.

Recipients will have varying degrees of understanding of our mission objective, including having no understanding of it at all, so this will dictate their reaction to our actions and their consequences. By this, I mean that someone who is introspective because they are on their own dedicated "spiritual" journey is likely to be more willing to understand, forgive, and show compassion compared with someone who is so deep in their own self-cherishing they can't see past their middle finger held up to us.

These distinctions among recipients may seem reminiscent of those we discussed earlier in regard to metta, or lovingkindness, practice. While they are defined by similar terminology and share similar characteristics, in the context of metta practice, the focus is on our practice of giving and how the different types of receivers affect our effort and ability to give, whereas, with the different types of recipients, the focus is on addressing their ability to accept what is given.

The teaching then goes deeper by addressing the quality of the relationship and how it affects the recipient's engagement with us in respect to their willingness or reluctance to accept what we give.

Allies, Neutrals, and Combatants

Let's look more closely at the quality of the relationships we might have with the different types of recipients. In keeping with the bodyguard metaphor, I've identified them as **allies**, **neutrals**, and **combatants**.

Allies

By allies, I do not mean only family or friends but a person who is living their life in a like-minded fashion (one of pursuing "spiritual" transformation and liberation) who, due to a deeper exploration of and insight into themselves and of life itself, is more understanding, forgiving, and receptive to our actions and has a desire for healthy interaction with us by reciprocating with being helpful and giving.

Neutrals

By neutral I do not mean uncaring or indifferent. A neutral person cares, but at times is like-minded and at other times is not. While capable, they simply are not as committed to a deeper exploration of the self as we are, or seriously committed to a spiritual pursuit, and due to this respond as such, with neither too much affirmation nor too much adversity. A neutral person lives their life as sometimes being helpful and sometimes not, but is never purposely harmful.

Combatants

By combatant, I do not mean only someone who has disdain for us personally. In the broader context, a combatant is simply anyone who is not on a deeper journey, and who has no interest in putting any effort into sharing our experience in a positive way, which in turn makes any interaction with them negative. Sadly, at their worst, a combatant will purposely act harmfully, and at their best be so selfish and self-involved they simply have no regard for others. While an ally is a giver, a combatant is a taker. (It is also important to understand that we can all be any one of these types at any time, so we must tread lightly!)

With these distinctions in mind, our personal relationship with any one of these types of recipient determines the strength of our tactical application of karma.

The traditional teachings say that we will have a stronger application of our actions and derive more benefit from them if the recipient is not only a like-minded ally but a past benefactor of ours, or has a personal importance for us, such as a family member, friend, parent, or teacher. Likewise, we will also have a stronger application of our actions and derive greater benefit from them with a neutral benefactor, family member, or friend, and even an enemy who once was a benefactor, friend, or even a family member.

Simply put, having been positively involved at one time, on any level, for any duration with someone can often be a theater for greater mission success. But on the other hand, interaction with someone we have only been negatively involved with will have a high risk of casualty.

It's important to note that working with karma involves not only dealing with the harm we've caused ourselves and are attempting to escape but also harm we have caused others with our harmfully conditioned actions. This will likely cause them to respond to us based on that negative experience, regardless of how we are interacting with them in the present. They are not a willing recipient, and this is embedded in their history with us and remains the norm for their interaction with us.

This is similar to what I teach people in personal protection seminars. I tell my seminar participants that I have done thousands of hours of surveillance and that the consistent issue I have experienced in every case is that the subject always follows a predictable routine. They often don't believe me when I tell them that even after I have done only one day of surveillance, I am able to gather enough information on the subject that when I come back days, weeks, or even months later, I can successfully predict what the person will do before they do it.

As uncomfortable as it is to hear, we are all creatures of habit, which makes us extremely vulnerable to an assailant. I'm not only referring to an unknown stalker deciding to creepily follow you around and learn your routine. In fact, statistics support the fact that victims know their attacker, or better put, the attacker knows *them*. Yes, sometimes personally, but more often through proximity. It could be someone who works in the same office building, or interacts with you through seemingly normal, innocent, harmless activity, such as working out at the same gym you do. It's not too difficult for someone who knows you will be at the gym every day at 8 a.m. in the morning to identify your vehicle, get your license plate, follow you to work or home or both, and so forth... You get the idea.

Using this personal protection teaching as a metaphor for Buddhist practice, the point that I'm making is that our harmful conditioning creates a predictable routine of harmful behavior that the people with whom we interact become familiar with and come to expect from us.

The more frequent the interaction is, the more accustomed they become to it. As they become more accustomed to it they come to expect it, which causes them to have a heightened level of expectation about our harmful behavior. That, in turn, triggers a quicker and more detrimental response from them when it happens, or even when they just think it's going to happen. Our problem then becomes that we only see them lashing out at us and hold it against them by classifying them as "enemies," rather than seeing their actions as an understandable, defensive response to *our* habitual, harmful actions.

While it is beneficial when any of these recipients is receptive to our tactical application of the practice, in my experience it is most beneficial when applied toward a difficult person or enemy. That is because it requires a more rigorous application over a sustained period of time, and having to dig deeper into myself to apply more patience, understanding, acceptance, compassion, and forgiveness has benefitted me by deepening my resolve and dedication to my mission. You could say that going deeper into enemy territory, engaging in a harder-fought battle, and emerging victorious has made the result that much more rewarding.

So now that you have been sworn in as a "karmic law enforcement officer," let me brief you on the most important aspect of your patrol duty—namely, being a peace officer, protecting and serving the public, and keeping the peace.

11

Tactics of Interdepending

Until this point, I've written at great length about the bodyguard protecting their client and each of us protecting our own inner Buddha; however, rarely, if ever, is the job done by a single person, even if they are an elite, special forces bodhisattva.

The bodyguard always has a support team. Likewise, the bodhisattva, or as I like to say, the Buddhist Peace Officer, always has their commanding officer (teacher/guru) and peace force (sangha) ready at the peace station (zendo) for backup.

When a bodyguard assignment has a high level of threat, the best course of action is to keep the subject in a secured, fortified, unknown location. Sometimes this is exactly the plan, but many times the subject is a high-profile person who cannot be isolated and has a responsibility to come out in public. We hear our leaders say that if we give into our fear the enemies win, and it is no different for us as we practice. If we give in to our fear, the near enemies win.

We may try to isolate ourselves from the pain and disappointment that accompanies the inherent unsatisfactory nature of life, and at times we do. But what we find is that it is just a temporary fix that ultimately makes us more vulnerable to the suffering we think we are hiding from. We all know that wherever we go we bring ourselves with us, and often we can be our own worst enemy!

Like the high-profile notorious VIP who must do their duty regardless of the threat involved, we too must take the risk and "do our duty."

This means engaging life, knowing the risks, but also knowing that the reward is worth it. But we do not do it alone.

As we investigate *interdependence* (that all existence is relational and dependent on something else), we see that our inner Buddha's protection is not only dependent on our relationship with our own conditioning, as I touched upon earlier in the Twelve Links of Origination) but also on our conditioned relationships with others, and that our existence depends as much on those around us as theirs does upon us.

This understanding directs our focus—not only in how we live our lives but how we live our lives in relation to others, which, in turn, dictates how our lives are equally affected by how they live their lives in relation to us. Most of us have heard the saying that one must clean up their own backyard before they attempt to clean up the world, and while poignantly true, when kept in a healthy balance, cleaning up the world also makes our own backyard even brighter.

The result of realizing interdependence is to see the role that duality plays in our lives. Doing so reveals the false separations we have created, and the tensions that arise from them. At the root of our problem is our attachment to the false notion that contradictory views cannot exist simultaneously with truths, and our mistaken belief that all paradoxes must be reconciled.

Being a Good Buddhist

One of the biggest separations many Buddhists must deal with is that of being Buddhist. Buddhism teaches us that we must investigate our deeply held beliefs—that while we need labels and constructs to manage our lives, we must not be attached to them and avoid being too idealistic and making everything black and white.

This seems easy at first, because we tend to begin our practice by dividing things into what we determine as being Buddhist or not Buddhist. We determine what a Buddhist should and should not do, and then we define ourselves based on that understanding. We create a mold for being a Buddhist and force ourselves to fit into it. This is not to say that our definition is inaccurate or not helpful, but in our quest to be a super-Buddhist, we often end up with an unhealthy attachment to an unrealistic expectation. This can be startling, as we ask ourselves how can trying to be good… be bad?

There are as many different definitions of what a "good" Buddhist is as there are Buddhist practitioners, but there are a few that most seem to share. It seems that to be an upstanding member in the Buddhist club, there are certain political, social, ecological, and lifestyle positions that we must all be on board with. Since I've brought up such a sensitive topic, it's only fair that I throw myself under the bus, so here is my list of not only what I thought constitutes a good Buddhist but what I thought defined the entry requirements to even *start* being a Buddhist. Period.

In my mind you had to be a bleeding-heart liberal, anti-war, anti-gun, vegan, social-service advocate, who protected a woman's right to choose, who worked for the environment, and stood up against racism and sexism and for LGBT equality, the poor, the hungry, and worked in an occupation that served others, was selfless, and low paying.

Now before you scream, "Are you saying you are not in agreement with these issues?" actually, I just defined myself *exactly*. What I am saying is that attachment to these seemingly noble issues is what is unhealthy.

Let me share a story that relates to this. We are all aware of the horrific trend of unarmed African Americans being shot and killed by white officers. You do not have to be a Buddhist to be outraged by this; however, most Buddhists I know are so attached to their rage they have placed the blame on *all* law enforcement officers rather than just the ones who are responsible, causing them to form a general negative judgment of *all* based on a *few*. Yet these same Buddhists will attack people for saying that *all* Muslims are terrorists, when of course they are not.

Here's the story I promised to illustrate my point.

> A good friend of mine is a combat veteran and a long-time law enforcement officer in a city where violence is a routine occurrence. One day he responded to a call about a knife-wielding man who had already killed someone and was holding several others hostage. Without a thought for his own safety, my friend entered the residence, subdued the knife-wielding assailant without injuring him or even drawing his own weapon, and saved the hostages' lives.
>
> After this harrowing experience he understandably needed to decompress, so he drove his police cruiser and parked by the beach, opened his windows to get some much-needed fresh air, and sat back, breathed deeply, and let the stress dissipate. As he was doing this, he remembered a detail about the incident he wasn't sure he had put in his notes, which he had already given to a detective. Always a diligent, by-the-book guy, he grabbed his phone and immediately texted the detail to the detective. As he was texting the point of fact to the fellow officer, a group of hipster dudes walked by and one said, "Fuckin' cops. Getting paid to fucking sit on his phone and do nothing!"

We all can get stuck in our deeply held beliefs, and when we do, our life is then defined by moments when we are constantly defending and exhorting the concepts and labels we use to navigate non-duality and multiplicity, relative and absolute, sameness and difference, form and emptiness, self and other, us and them, mine and yours, good and bad, right and wrong, countries, borders, flags, religion, race, gender, and so on. Life becomes a tedious, exhausting, frustrating, disheartening fight, where everyone is simultaneously trying to prove themselves *right,* which in turn makes everyone simultaneously respond to prove how they are not *wrong.*

Buddhist teaching responds to this dilemma by teaching us how to find a balance between realizing both perspectives. When the teachings say that "everything is one," it's important to note that that also includes that everything is also *not* one. That experiencing non-duality is not the act of eradicating differences or blurring the view of duality; it's experiencing not *needing* to, as we intrinsically understand that any effort to negate or confirm is the basis of our attachment and thus our suffering.

An old koan teaching says: "Things are not as they seem. Nor are they otherwise."

To understand this we must recognize the coexistence of truth, and how it leads to stability. This stability is not only the ability to stand firmly between these two seemingly opposing truths but also to stand firmly upon them.

The famous Zen master Dogen explains the process of cultivating this ability in the following verse explaining the Five Ranks:

> *To study the Buddha way is to study the self.*
> *To study the self is to forget the self.*
> *To forget the self is to be actualized by the myriad of things.*
> *When actualized by the myriad of things, your body and mind*
> *as well as the body and mind of others will drop away.*
> *No trace of realization remains and this no-trace continues endlessly.*

As we "study the self," we see that our attachment to our deeply held beliefs, and the patterns of habitual behaviors that come from them, have caused us to misunderstand ourselves, and we begin to clearly see the construct of a false self we have created.

As a result of this investigation we "forget the self" by letting go of our identification with the construct we had created, which frees us from the constraints of our self-cherishing perspective.

It is then that we are "actualized by the myriad of things," as we see ourselves in others, and see others as ourselves. Where form, emptiness, birth and death, this and that, intertwine, as everything is one, and one is everything. Where we experience our place within the interconnectedness and impermanence of all things, knowing that change is the only constant. We know that we are unique in our existence, yet we know that it is others that make our existence unique.

We know this, not as knowledge but as intrinsic truth resulting from experience that thoroughly permeates every fiber of our being. There is no separation, as "no trace of realization remains and this no-trace continues endlessly," as we live with a spontaneous ease, an expansive openness, free from any attachment to self, other, or circumstance.

A koan explains this rather simply: "It is like someone in the middle of the dark night reaching for a pillow."

We all know what it's like to reach for our pillow in the middle of the night. It is an intuitive act that spontaneously happens from complete oneness of mind and body, and it is carried out without a hint of thought or self-consciousness that would separate the self and the act. We do so with our whole unified being. No doer, no deed; just an act of natural, selfless, complete compassion. This attainment is the highest rank, or better put, the actions of the person of *no* rank.

To be a person of "no rank" means that we do not live with a sense of superiority, arrogance, and entitlement or a feeling of inferiority or lack of worth within ourselves. It means to live free from ego attachment, having no need to prove oneself or be recognized in any esteem. To have no need to judge ourselves against an idea of self, or to compare ourselves with others.

To be a person of no rank, we must go through the different evolving ranks to get there. I've used the metaphor of a police officer going through departmental ranks to help explain this. Though I use the term "peace officer" as a play on words for Buddhist purposes, wouldn't it be great if they were actually called that!

The longer the Buddhist Peace Officer walks the beat and keeps the peace, the more they will be rewarded by their chief with commendations for service excellence, as well as being promoted in rank. This ascent in position comes from their dedicated interaction with the people they serve. This dedication stems from the Buddhist Peace Officer's desire to cultivate an understanding of their situation, as well as the intent to build a stronger relationship with them to better serve and protect them.

THE FIVE RANKS OF THE BUDDHIST PEACE OFFICER

The Buddhist Peace Officer understands that to serve the community, they are not on a separate patrol *of* the community, but stationed *within* it, and that this makes them *part* of that community. The higher in rank that they go, the more engaged that they are with the community and the more engaged that they are with the peace officer. The five ranks of attainment the Buddhist Peace Officer can achieve are:

Patrolman

At this rank the Buddhist Peace Officer is a cadet just out of the academy, a rookie on probation. While trained in basic tactics and having tactical knowledge, they have no real world experience in applying it. As they gain on-the-job experience, they see the nature of how application works and begin to feel more secure and confident in their role within the community. At this rank, their focus is personal, completely on themselves and their ability to do the job. To be a good officer at this point means to constantly be observing and evaluating themself within the context of their actions. In Buddhist terms, this reflects experiencing the relative within the absolute. Meaning one is beginning to see oneself differently and realizing that there is a new way to respond to the typical experiences of everyday life. In Dogen's words, "To study the Buddha way is to study the self."

Sergeant

At this rank the Buddhist Peace Officer is no longer a rookie who is solely focused on their own performance. Their experience is broadening their focus to have the ability to see the role the community as a whole plays in their personal ability to do the job. Their focus begins to expand, as they see a bigger picture, one in which they examine the community's role in their actions, which now supersedes their personal inclinations in their own choice of actions. In Buddhist terms, this reflects experiencing the absolute within the relative. In Dogen's words, "To study the self is to forget the self."

Lieutenant

At this rank the Buddhist Peace Officer is becoming a seasoned, experienced officer. Their view is completely focused on the community and its well-being, even at times at their own expense. In Buddhist terms, this reflects experiencing the absolute. In Dogen's words, "To forget the self is to be actualized by the myriad of things."

Captain

At this rank, the Buddhist Peace Officer is a veteran officer who has been through many difficult situations. Their view has broadened to consider and balance their personal role in seamless harmony with the role of the community in directing their style of protecting and serving the community. They now see no separation between themself and the community. In Buddhist terms, this reflects experiencing the relative and the absolute. In Dogen's words, "When actualized by the myriad of things, your body and mind as well as the body and mind of others will drop away."

Chief

At this rank, the Buddhist Peace Officer is a commanding officer whose experience has given them the maturity of not needing to weigh the needs of the community with those of the department's, as they have now become perfectly integrated. They now act with complete spontaneity motivated by wise intention, which arises from intrinsic wisdom that has been cultivated while going through the previous ranks. In Buddhist terms, this reflects experiencing the unity of relative and absolute. In Dogen's words, "No trace of realization remains and this no-trace continues endlessly."

The Buddhist teacher Thich Nhat Hanh has coined the term "inter-being" to reflect this reconciling of our inner self with the way that things are *outside* ourselves. As he so poetically says, "inter-being" is when we have achieved complete integration of both the perspectives of relative and absolute, of self and other into our actions, with no separation. Doing so will result in the realization that we all "inter-are," and when we truly realize we "inter-are," we cannot help but "inter-be."

As I am always focused on how to "do" Buddhism, I key in on his use of this term as a verb, as for me inter-being requires us to clearly know what we must "inter-do." This "inter-doing" hinges upon holding in our minds specific tenets. These tenets are much more than just knowledge, or a mental commitment to specific actions. They are a permeating state of mind from which all intentions rise and from which all movement takes place.

As the Sixth Patriarch Hui Neng said, "Flag does not move. Wind does not move. Mind moves."

And as the Buddha said, "Deeds exist, though no doer can be found."

So now I will brief you on how to "inter-do," as I outline the tactics implemented by an engaged Buddhist.

12

Tactically Engaged Buddhism

While engaged Buddhism is considered an evolved, modern spin on an ancient practice, when investigated, one can see that it actually is a logical progression for traditional Buddhist practice to take.

With regard to the bodhisattva's vow to save all beings, engaged Buddhism's mission is to use the dharma (Buddhist teachings) as social action to eradicate social, political, environmental, and economic injustice and the suffering that results from it.

Thich Nhat Hanh has outlined 14 precepts of engaged Buddhism. I've borrowed from him the ones I think best fit my use of the bodyguard tactics metaphor. I am calling these "The Buddhist Bodyguard's Code of Tactical Engagement."

Do Not Be Bound to Any Doctrine, Theory, or Ideology

The success of a bodyguard detail or a personal protection scenario rests not on relying on a conceptual strategy or a static technique but in the ability to assess the situation as it unfolds and adapt to it appropriately. While training is an imperative foundation, its application develops as a result of challenging that training under the threat of different conditions arising.

The Buddhist teachings direct us to continually question our beliefs and break attachment to our fixed ideas. The Buddha said that we should not take his word for it, that we should investigate our direct experience and find out for ourselves, while the Dalai Lama says that if any teaching in Buddhism is proven wrong it should be abandoned. This indicates an attitude not found often in religion, namely, a flexible, open-mindedness that is not blindly beholden to a particular dogma. Having a conviction in what one believes is fine, but to not be able to alter or change that conviction and the actions it dictates is exactly the attachment the teachings stress is at the root of our suffering.

This is of the utmost importance, as while studying *what* to do is imperative, applying it comes from testing it under circumstances that are *not* conducive for it. This goes to a deeper point, which I addressed earlier, of being able to adapt our tactical application, as it addresses our ability to adapt our perspective and have flexibility within that perspective. This not only enables us to see that our tactics need to be adapted but have the willingness to do so.

First and foremost, a change of perspective is about being able to assess that a specific situation mandates a different tactical response rather than having to identify a certain tactic as not being applicable.

Sometimes adapting tactics involves simply choosing a different tool from our standard toolbox. More importantly, it involves our ability to modify the application of the tool we have for it to be an appropriate response, as well as understanding that we need to identify which of our tried-and-true tools are no longer efficient and need to be replaced by new ones.

DO NOT THINK THAT YOUR KNOWLEDGE IS ABSOLUTE TRUTH

As I discussed earlier, it is imperative for the bodyguard to gather intelligence in order to ensure mission success. At the same time, the bodyguard is ready at any moment to disregard it due to a security survey or threat assessment, identifying conditions that contradict that intelligence. This is the same as the Dalai Lama directing practitioners to abandon any Buddhist teaching that is proven to be wrong as a result of direct experience.

While Buddhism does speak of absolute truth, what I am referring to here is that the relative truth we must decipher in the management of our moment-to-moment lives is an ever-changing experience that constantly ebbs and flows, causing what we know to either gain or lose relevance, not in its validity but in its usefulness in the context of each different moment.

Just as a protection agent must always investigate intelligence and vet it as either viable intel or the propaganda of a campaign of misinformation led by the near enemy operatives, Buddha's bodyguard must always be diligent in investigating conditions, causes, effects, and intentions and the insight that stems from them. As the conditions change, so must the insight, and sometimes, the insight must be abandoned completely, because the conditions were incorrectly assessed and the insight was actually rooted in misinformation.

Do Not Maintain Anger

Bodyguards are trained to make intellectual assessments of their circumstances and to respond to them with concise, efficient, and appropriate tactics that are free from the subjective bias of emotional entanglement.

The Buddha taught to *cause no harm,* but this teaching is often also, in my opinion, wrongly interpreted as *use no force.* (In my first book, *Fighting Buddha,* I devoted a whole chapter to the issue of a Buddhist practitioner reconciling the Buddha's teaching of causing no harm with the use of force, so if you'd like to delve deeper into that issue please check it out. Because of this, I'll just briefly touch on the subject here.)

The reason I am bringing up the issue of reconciling the Buddha's teaching of *cause no harm* with the use of force in a section titled "Do not maintain anger" is because most people, whether Buddhist or not, associate anger with force or violence.

When a protection agent uses force, they do so from a clear assessment that results in well-intended, appropriate actions to stop a violent threat against their client. In fact, any emotional imbalance, especially anger, would be extremely detrimental to a successful threat response, which requires the calm and precision that come with being mentally and emotionally in balance.

That is why a protection agent always trains techniques under the stress simulation of a real-life scenario. Training under conditions least conducive to the scenario is the only way to learn to realistically apply techniques in the most efficient manner. Experiencing the stress triggers the unbalance of our mental and emotional states, and in that way we learn to balance them.

In a Buddhist context I define harm, violence, or in this case anger, as being rooted in ignorance, which results in harmful action fueled by harmful intention, meaning the desire to victimize. I define use of force as being rooted in wisdom, resulting in helpful action inspired by compassionate intention to stop violence and prevent victimization. So, with this in mind, we can understand that the directive of tactical engagement to *not maintain anger* is directing us that we should instead engage with equanimity and lovingkindness.

At one time I directed crisis response in the emergency room and psychiatric ward of a major hospital. It was my responsibility to be the first responder to any situation involving a disruptive, non-compliant, or violent person. This involved employing tactics ranging from verbally defusing a potential altercation to physically restraining someone. Not a day went by that I wasn't dealing with a patient or family member in the midst of losing control and acting out. Most of these situations would involve a mentally ill patient who was physically acting out and needed to be restrained for their own safety, as well as for the safety of those around them.

Let me share with you a particular experience from my time in that position that sticks out in my mind as exemplifying the tactic of *not maintaining anger* and instead, engaging with equanimity and loving-kindness.

When not doing a walking tour of the emergency room or psychiatric ward, or not responding to a situation, I was stationed at a post at the emergency room entrance where police and paramedics would bring patients in. Often, patients were brought in screaming and cursing, either rolled in by paramedics strapped to a gurney or being walked in by the police with their hands cuffed behind them—so often, in fact, that it became normal to me.

One day, while I was sitting at this post, both the police and paramedics were bringing in a guy whose arms and legs were handcuffed to the gurney. Nothing new about that, but what shocked me was seeing that the guy had a seven-inch knife penetrating his forearm, with the handle on top of his arm and the full length of the blade sticking out from the underside. As if this wasn't enough, I was taken back that rather than screaming or yelling like most patients, the guy was laughing! Add to this that one of the officers told me that he had stabbed himself, and I was aghast.

He was quickly taken to the surgical wing, and I expected to see him up on the psychiatric ward eventually, but a few days later, I was surprised to find the guy lying unrestrained in a bed in the regular part of the emergency room.

When I inquired about the situation, I was told that there were no beds available in the lockdown ward and that they were waiting for one to become available. The supervising doctor had agreed with the psychiatrist that the patient's lack of a violent history meant that he could be managed in the ward just by keeping him medicated.

I didn't agree, but it wasn't my call. In fact, most of the situations I had to handle were a consequence of mismanaged treatment of the patient. As it turned out, this one would be no different.

Over the course of the next several days, as I took my periodic tours around the emergency room, I got to know him a bit. I was impressed to find out that he was not only an Iraqi war vet but a former special forces team member. He shared with me that his mental illness had forced him out of the service and caused a downward spiral ever since. He was very vocal about hating being on medication; this incident was the result of him choosing to stop taking his.

Throughout our conversations, I noticed that his ability to be lucid and his demeanor and mood were constantly shifting. This was a dynamic I had seen before with other patients, the result of doctors experimenting with different combinations of medication in an effort to find the best course of treatment for each patient. Unfortunately for the patient, this is a harrowing process, and it was no different for him. I watched him bounce back and forth from high to low, and observed his agitation begin to build as a result. It didn't surprise me when I was called into the ER as a precaution when he was yelling at a nurse.

This happened several times, and each time I was able to befriend him, earn his trust, and calm him down. With each incident, I could see further deterioration in him, and finally it all came to a head.

I was called into the ER to find he had gotten out of bed and was standing in the middle of the ER with his IV stand in tow, arguing incoherently with a doctor.

Suddenly he exploded, and in a blink of an eye, his hands were firmly around the doctor's neck. As he pushed him to the ground, I ran and grabbed him from the back in what's called a "seat belt grip," which is one hand over his shoulder and one hand under his shoulder clasped on his chest, and pulled him backwards off the doctor.

Usually at this point I could hold a patient still so that a nurse could inject him with medication, but this 5-foot-3-inch, 130-pound ex-special forces guy was no joke! Add to the situation that his IV had ripped out of his arm and blood was everywhere, I was just able to restrain him enough to give my backup time to arrive. Once they did, it took three of us to get him into restraints. Once in restraints, he was medicated and whisked up to the lockdown psychiatric ward.

Several weeks later I was sitting at my ER post and was shocked to see him walking down the hall toward me, smiling and looking great. He approached me and offered his hand to shake. As I shook it, his expression got deathly serious. "I am so sorry I caused you any problems. I hope you are okay, and I deeply apologize for my actions." I accepted his apology and watched him walk out to the street and out of view.

To be perfectly honest, just because I was able to deal with this situation and others like it with calm professionalism does not mean that it was easy. The reality is that when someone is acting out and you have to physically intervene, it's quite hard to not take it personally. The trick is actually to avoid trying. Just like we let our thoughts come and go during our meditation practice, the trick to not "carry anger" is to realize that anger is actually a normal response that will inevitably arise, especially in this type of situation, and that we simply should acknowledge it and not attach to it.

So, during an altercation, just as we do in meditation, we bring our focus back to our breath to keep from being swept away by our random thoughts and getting lost in a narrative we add that is rooted in what we think about our experience. Instead, the protection agent brings his attention to the protocol he is directed to follow, and does not get swept away in an anger reaction or start a negative, harmful narrative about it. This is two-fold, as it not only keeps the agent safe but the threatening subject safe as well.

This protocol is also like Buddhist practice in directing the agent to treat the subject with kindness, respect, and dignity while in the midst of an altercation. This is accomplished by using non-injurious, diffusal tactics to control and de-escalate the conflict, while at the same time using a sedate, non-threatening tone and polite language to calm the subject.

This is not just about *how* the subject is spoken to but also the content of *what* is said. Not only is the agent saying "please, sir" when asking the subject to comply and "thank you, sir" when they do but also explaining what is happening to the subject. So, after the agent has secured a restraining lock on the subject, he would then initiate the step of walking the client away by saying, "Sir, please relax. I'm now going to escort you back to your room and wait with you for the doctor to see you." As the subject complied and began walking, the agent would add, "Thank you for cooperating, sir. I truly appreciate your help." On the walk back to the subject's room, the agent would try to further put the subject at ease with supportive conversation like, "Don't worry, sir. Everyone is here to help you. Everything will be alright."

Of course, what I just described takes place when the subject is compliant. It rarely goes that smoothly, but regardless of how it goes, the agent must maintain the same decorum. Here's another story from when I was running the emergency room psychiatric security pertaining to not carrying anger in a situation that was extremely difficult not to.

I was in the emergency room when a patient had escaped from the long-term locked ward, which was located on another floor. When I got the call on my radio, the patient had last been observed running out of a hospital side door. I ran out the nearest door to where I was stationed, just in time to see him trying to cross the busy street about half a block away from me.

As I sprinted toward him, he turned his head as he checked the traffic flow, saw me, and bolted. I finally caught up to him about a block away. I grabbed his arm and instantly applied a wrist lock, which caused him to scream. (Now before you freak out about it, let me say that while it does hurt, the technique I used had very little risk of injury to him. The thing about pain compliance locks is that the first experience is the worst, as the more you feel it the more used to it you get. Having had it applied to me thousands of times over the last 25 years, my threshold has increased dramatically in how I can withstand them.)

Having secured my restraining lock, I then gave him verbal commands to remain calm and stay still, and explained that I was going to escort him back to the hospital. He was calm and compliant and walked willingly with me. As we got closer to the hospital, he told me that his wrist hurt and politely asked me to loosen my grip. Feeling bad for him I did just a bit, which gave him just enough mobility to suddenly turn toward me and try to bite my face. In response I cranked the lock down, and he screamed even louder than before.

"Sorry, sir," I said to him, as he walked on his tippy toes (a reflex to the pain), back into the hospital with me. "I really wish that you had remained calm and there was no need for me to do this. But try to relax. I know this hurts, but this escort technique will not cause you any injury. You will be okay, and I will let go as soon as we get you back to the unit."

He seemed to calm down and get more at ease the more I spoke, and I was able to get him safely back into the locked ward, and the situation ended without any further incident.

Explaining yourself and your actions to the subject is vital, as not under-standing what is happening to them is usually what the subject is most fearful of. By including them in the process, explaining to them what's happening, and affording them the choice to comply, as opposed to forcing them to comply, not only puts the subject at much greater ease but calms the agent, the situation, and all others involved as well.

Much like how an agent who is focused on safety and security proto-col is able to calmly stay focused on the task at hand, a Buddhist practi-tioner being focused on the task at hand of being mindful and following the conduct commitments is able to not be overwhelmed by conditioned thinking and reactivity and is calmly able to not *carry anger*.

Be Present

I've already discussed mindfulness at great length earlier in the book. It is a vital part of the foundation of Buddhist practice that is addressed frequently in Buddhist teaching, so I understand that it might seem odd to need a directive that further addresses the need to be "present." I am discussing it here, though, as it relates to *dispersion*, which refers to not merely a lack of concentration but the quality of the concentration that is present.

Think about how we take part in a new activity. It could be any activity, not just Buddhist practice. When we start something new, we usually do so with enthusiasm and vigor, so much so, in fact, that the experience we have is so gratifying and rewarding it is almost overwhelm-ing. We become consumed when doing it, completely engulfed in it, with no separation between subject and object, no observer; we simply *are* the activity.

But after participating in this activity over and over, we find that while we might be present and engaging in the activity, the quality of our concentration has diminished to a point where there *is* separation, where we notice the break between subject and object, where we find ourselves on the outside observing, and even judging the inferior results of our doing. We are able to see that while concentration has engaged us in the activity, the diminishing of its quality has reduced the effort within the concentration to merely a going-through-the-motions routine.

I'll use an example from my own practice to elaborate this point. Every morning when I meditate, I also say aloud specific teachings to remind myself of my aspirations for my practice and recite commitments to take specific actions in my practice to support my aspirations. I remember being shocked the first time I was able to see the diminished quality of my concentration. I realized that while I had started my recitation practice strongly, and that I still had a level of concentration that was strong enough to keep me reciting it, I was also deep in thought about a jujitsu technique I wanted to work on in that morning's training.

The most shocking part of the experience was that in spite of my thinking about jujitsu and not paying attention to my recitation, when I "tuned back in" to what I was reciting, I hadn't missed a beat. I was still reciting perfectly and was at the exact point I would have been in the sequence had I not thought about jujitsu at all! It was as if I had been completely present the whole time! The experience felt like there were two of me, doing two different things at the same time, with neither version of me fully invested in either.

So to deal with dispersion, to be present, you must be able to realize you're not.

RESOLVE ALL CONFLICTS

I spoke earlier about "hardening the target," which entailed how we must investigate our security breaches and secure them. But that was in the context of our proactive action to prevent *new* threats. But what about our *old* threats, the ones we are well aware of? If we do not address these unresolved conflicts, they will always be lurking as threats to which we will always be vulnerable. But in this context, rather than just securing ourselves by hunkering down in a secure bunker to shut these threats out and avoid them, to deal with our unresolved conflicts we must venture out of our secure comfort zone and address the threat face to face. While at first assessment, this directive references our need to let go of resentment and forgive those who have threatened us, at its deepest level this directive is most often about our need to surrender, as it is *we* that need to seek forgiveness for *our* past attacks on *them*.

Speak Truthfully and Courageously

As I mentioned earlier, in the discussion of Wise Speech in the context of the Eightfold Tactical Path, silence can be the most harmful misuse of speech. This directive mandates that we must have the courage to say what needs to be said, at the moment it needs to be said, regardless of the consequence. This goes deeper than merely sharing our feelings and addressing our own issues. This is a mandate to be a voice for others who have none. It is a directive that we address injustice whenever and wherever we see it.

Take a Clear Stand

The old saying "You'd better stand for something, or you're gonna fall for anything" is not just a cliché; it is actually an on-point directive. I've already discussed the importance of being clear about our intentions, but in this context what I am talking about is being clear about the issue our intentions support. If where we stand on an issue is muddled and confused, and we have not clearly identified our mission objective, then the actions we take end up obscuring it, rather than clarifying it, both to ourselves and to others.

Do Not Benefit from Suffering

A bodyguard has an ethical responsibility to their client. This responsibility ranges from keeping them safe (of course) to maintaining privacy and discretion about the client's personal life. To not put the client and these issues first is a dereliction in duty, with sometimes fatal results. This also means to put them before your employment.

For a bodyguard to not intervene in a situation they believe to be harmful to the client simply because they think they would be fired for doing so amounts to malpractice. Before a bodyguard chooses to not intervene for selfish reasons, thereby putting their client at risk, the ethical thing to do would be for the bodyguard to resign. It is in the best interests of the bodyguard, as well as the client, to do so, to protect the bodyguard from being implicated in the consequences for *not* having intervened.

Too often a bodyguard has stood by and done nothing as their client indulged in life-threatening alcoholism or drug addiction, sexual deviance, dangling babies over balconies, and so on (sorry, while I was a huge MJ fan, there was no excusing that behavior or his security team's tolerance of it). For a bodyguard to allow the client to put themselves in jeopardy because they do not want to risk losing a paycheck is reprehensible.

Most people just think of the physical aspect of protecting the client, but more frequently, the bodyguard is protecting the client from their own harmful indulgences and the way they can be exploited by others. Embarrassing or incriminating pictures or videos are too often sold to the highest bidder, or worse, used to blackmail a client.

Like a bodyguard, in Buddhist practice, we must always be directed by an accurate moral compass. I have discussed the five basic precepts found in most traditions, but Zen actually has ten precepts, including one that states, "One should never have personal gain at the expense of another."

RESPECT THE BODY

This directive touches many areas of practice, ranging from physical fitness and mental and emotional wellness to the directive of not misusing sexuality I discussed earlier in relation to the conduct directives. In this context I will address the fitness, health, and wellness aspect, as I feel that it is a much neglected subject in Buddhism.

Simply put, all the training and tactical ability in the world doesn't matter if there is not the physical ability to support its application. No matter how skilled a bodyguard is, if they cannot physically respond those skills are useless. It is no different for the Buddhist practitioner, as the state of our physical condition is directly tied in to the mental and emotional states our actions are rooted in. Successful Buddhist practice entails having the self-discipline to take the action needed to balance our physical and mental states and the result of having achieved that balance.

You may think that by following all of the protocols and directives I have laid out in this book, you will develop a complete skillset and mastery of its application—mission accomplished. But nothing could be farther from the truth. No matter how many conflicts we come through, the battle never ends. So now let me give you your standing orders on why and how we need to carry on our mission indefinitely.

13

MISSION *NOT* ACCOMPLISHED

J ust as the bodyguard's mission does not end with the successful conclusion of engaging a threat incident, nor does the Buddhist practitioner's path end with a singular, enlightened, meditative experience. While these isolated incidents are vitally important, moving, and transformational, no matter how exhilarating they may be, they are still just temporary moments based on temporary conditions that will pass.

For both bodyguard and Buddhist, such experiences are doubtless energizing and invigorating, fulfilling and validating. But while they may seem to represent the attainment of their ultimate goal—the reason for all their hard work and perseverance—they also teach us that not only must we get right back to work without a moment's hesitation but that our work never ends.

As a koan teaching tells us, "To touch the absolute is not yet enlightenment."

When these moments come, there is a tendency to think, "Aha, I've got it!" Yet, just as on one level this gratifying thought fills us with a sense of accomplishment and empowerment, on another level we can already feel it slipping away, as the moment passes, and we find ourselves facing a new one, with a completely different set of conditions and circumstances. We quickly learn that regardless of the depth of our insight or the level of skillfulness of our actions, each situation is different, mandating a different response from us each and every time.

It can be extremely dejecting to rise to the moment and handle a situation like an elite, special forces bodhisattva in one moment, only in the next moment to fall to the depths of being like a hungry ghost suffering in a hell realm. (A "hungry ghost" is a mythical figure in Buddhist folklore whose desires can never be satisfied. They are depicted as having a bloated stomach that constantly yearns for more, but because they have extremely thin necks and pinhole mouths, eating is extremely painful and difficult, and they can never take in enough to satisfy themselves.)

Using the example of a hungry ghost as a metaphor, we can see how it represents how we can be attached to, and completely driven by, the insatiable desires of our emotional needs in an extremely unhealthy way. This is why it is in the moments directly after experiencing the highest of "highs" that we need to be extremely careful, as the desire to cling to or pursue the experience can be overwhelming.

When we cling to the "high" experience of a past moment, we end up getting stuck in a state that is not applicable to the reality of the new moment, and we end up failing miserably in how we engage it and respond to it. The other conflict we face is that after the "high" experience has passed, we pursue it and try to replicate it, leading us to avoid the new reality in front of us. Either way we end up suffering miserably.

As another old Zen saying states, "While anyone can find peace at the top of a mountain, few can bring it back down with them to the village."

Which begs the question: Can we come down off that mountaintop and bring the experience we've discovered with us? Happily, the answer is yes, but to do so happens differently from the way we think it does.

Like I said, when we experience these exhilarating moments, it's very easy to get attached to them and shift the goal of our practice to holding onto them or chasing them, rather than letting them organically come and go. What we need to do is to use the moments immediately after these "highs" as motivation to recommit to the basic legwork that got us there in the first place, understanding that it's the journey that is most gratifying not the occasional extremes it takes us to, no matter how great they might be.

The irony is that if we chase these experiences we can never find them, but when we use them as motivation to deepen our resolve in our work, we see that they tend to come more and more often. And in another ironic twist, the more often they come, the less they seem to stand out as special, as they become the norm rather than a sporadic divergence.

It is this experience that teaches us that our mission is never completed. After the satisfaction of saving their client, the bodyguard knows that they must return to the mundane tasks that make up most of their job, and the Buddhist practitioner understands that they must return to the mundane circumstances and work with the nuisances that go on between these moments. (Yes, the bodyguard looks at successfully dealing with a threat as a high, just as a Buddhist would feel about the "high" of a blissful meditation moment.)

We must realize and accept that it is what's found in-between these moments that is truly the most important aspect of our work. What is most enlightening is to be able to sustain the same conviction in the teachings and the same resolve to practice them that arises from the "holy" moments, even amid the mundane moments.

The depth of resolve required to sustain this type of commitment is found in the first of the four Buddhist vows (or as I prefer to call it, commitments): *to save all beings.* Underpinning this commitment is the Buddhist operative's willingness to sacrifice their own entry into nirvana until they have completed the mission of evacuating all beings from samsara into nirvana. While most Buddhist teachers and practitioners, including myself, view this as a metaphor describing the depth of dedication and perseverance a practitioner needs to commit to, I also understand it as literally saying that our mission is never complete, meaning that we never reach an endpoint in our practice.

Contrary to what many, even long-term practitioners believe—nirvana, enlightenment, satori, waking up is not a singular event that once it happens becomes a permanent experience.

I am well aware that this contradicts many traditional teachings that define those states as the final rebirth from samsara and the permanent end to greed, hate, and delusion. But that has not been my experience, nor the experience of my teachers, nor for that matter of the Buddha himself, as I understand it.

Remember, the teachings speak of Mara attacking the Buddha right up till the moment of his death. So, with this in mind, we can understand these states as the ability to resist being threatened, rather than the permanent absence of being threatened. This is significant, as it demonstrates that these states are a shift *within* us, rather than any change in the nature of existence *outside* us.

Sadly, many practitioners mistakenly understand the purpose of their practice. They see it as the quest to attain these states for the purpose of permanently altering their state, rather than understanding that what led them to Buddhist practice in the first place was the suffering that arose from being in a constant altered state, as a result of identifying with a misunderstanding of the self, and the aversion and pursuits that came with it.

As they pursue these altered states as the end goal of their practice, they do not understand that they are repeating the exact same unhealthy behavior that got them into practice in the first place. They miss the point that even though they now have a "healthy" goal, they are still acting out of unhealthy intent. As a result, they complain that they haven't found "true enlightenment"; they do not see that what the

Buddhist path truly entails, what "true enlightenment" actually is, is *the end of pursuing an altered state.*

If you are lucky enough to experience this realization, always remember that Dogen said that this "end goes on endlessly."

So now that we have come to the end of this briefing on being Buddha's bodyguard, I will leave you with one last directive on how to proceed as the director of your own security detail.

Afterword

For me, Buddhism has never been something to *believe* in; it has always been something to *do*. In fact, I would say that Buddhism is not something one should believe in, but something they should always be putting to the test.

In my experience, putting my practice "to the test" has never resulted in deeper belief but greater doubt. This doubt is not rooted in my *not* having conviction in the teachings, nor the teachings *not* having a beneficial application. Quite the contrary. It's resulted in me doubting everything I *think* I know. Yes, after 30 years of Buddhist studies and practice, I am proud to say that most of the time, "I do not know."

As a Zen koan teaches:

> Hogen was going on a pilgrimage.
>
> Master Jizo asked, "Where are you going?"
>
> Hogen said, "Around on a pilgrimage."
>
> Master Jizo asked, "For what purpose?"
>
> Hogen said, "I do not know."
>
> Master Jizo said, "Not knowing is most intimate."
>
> Hearing this Hogen achieved great enlightenment.

To truly "not know" is the actualization of oneness, the seamlessness of direct experience. To "not know" is the ability to be free from the need to control our lives. It is the breaking of our attachment to the fixed ideas we hold that separate us from direct experience. We feel secure and stable when we hold onto our fixed ideas, so to let go of them takes great courage. When we do so, it feels like we are stepping off solid ground into a great abyss. As the great teacher Pema Chödrön often says, "There is never any solid ground upon which we can stand."

It is in this context that a koan asks us, "Standing atop a hundred foot pole, how do you proceed?"

To not know how to "proceed" is to step out of our emotional comfort zone and be willing to be open and vulnerable. This openness and vulnerability requires us to accept the present as it is, and let go of our regret of the past, and our fear of the future. We must step off our "solid" ground, step off the top of our hundred-foot pole, and take a great leap and seek and embrace uncertainty. It seems that we are taking a great risk, when we do so, but it is in letting go that we see just how much there is to hold onto, see that the true risk we take is to *not* let go and stay stuck.

To engage the unknown is the only thing we must know. We must put great faith in our doubt in order to truly know! I hope that, having finished reading this, I have truly helped you know much *less* than you did before you read it!

Suggested Reading

Das, Surya. *Awakening the Buddha Within: Tibetan Wisdom for the Modern World*. New York: Broadway Books, 1998.

Letting Go of the Person You Used To Be: Lessons on Change, Loss, and Spiritual Transformation. New York: Harmony Publications, 2004.

Gyatso, Kelsang. *Joyful Path of Good Fortune: The complete Buddhist Path to Enlightenment*. Ulverston, UK: Tharpa Publications, UK, 1990.

_____. *How to Solve Our Human Problems: The Four Noble Truths*. Ulverston, UK: Tharpa Publications, 2007.

Hanh, Thich Nhat. *Reconciliation: Healing the Inner Child*. Berkeley, CA: Parallax Press, 2010.

_____. *The Heart of the Buddha's Teaching: Transforming Suffering into Peace, Joy, and Liberation*. New York: Harmony Publishing, 2015.

Korda, Josh. *Unsubscribe: Opt out of Delusion and Tune In to the Truth*. Boston: Wisdom Publications, 2017.

Lama, Dalai. *How to Practice: The Way to a Meaningful Life*. New York: Atria Books, 2003.

_____. *The Universe in a Single Atom: The Convergence of Science and Spirituality*. New York: Harmony Publishing, 2006.

Thurman, Robert. *Inner Revolution: Life, Liberty, and the Pursuit of Happiness*. New York: Riverhead Books, 1999.

Warner, Brad. *It Came From Beyond Zen: More Practical Advice from Dogen, Japan's Greatest Zen Master*. Novato, CA: New World Library, 2017.

Young, Shinzen. *The Science of Enlightenment: How Meditation Works*. Boulder, CO: Sounds True, 2016.

Acknowledgments

There is a little known fifth vow for Buddhist authors that goes:

Unacknowledged beings are numberless,
I vow to acknowledge them all.

I n just what sutra this vow originated from is unclear, but what is clear, is that most Buddhist authors take this vow so seriously that they absolutely do attempt to acknowledge all beings. I have always been in awe of the authors that have pages of acknowledgements with hundreds of names. Or perhaps I'm simply jealous that they seem to be so tight with so many, many people when I have such a scant few that barely put up with me!

So with that said, while every single being that has crossed my path deserves an acknowledgement, as every interaction I've had surely has had an influence on this book, I'd like to simply give the proper shout outs of cred to the scant few that truly made an impact on this work.

First, thank you to Sabine Weeke, Nicky Leach and the crew at Findhorn Press that yet again not only believed in and supported my work, but did an amazing job turning the mess that I presented them into a great work of "art."

A huge shout out to those scant few that put up with me and whose support has been invaluable... Lisa Eisenberg, Rob Maddalone, Edward Alvarado, Kathy Nordone, Marci Tauber, Paul Kotch, Jeff Sokolowski and Jeffrey Rose.

Of course props to you the reader for supporting me, I truly do appreciate it!

And lastly a deep bow of gratitude to my teachers and fellow students of both the martial arts and Buddhism. To Professor Bill Scott and the crew at the BJJ Shore Academy in Pt. Pleasant, NJ for not only providing me with amazing training, but for your support and friendship off the mat as well. Shout out to Noah Levine and Josh Korda whose teachings still resonate with me in a most profound way some 15 years later, and to Geshe Wangdu and the crew at the Mahayana Sutra & Tantra center in Howell, NJ for the incredible teachings you share with me and the incredible amount of deep down, belly laughs we share every Sunday morning! Who the hell ever thought Tibetan Buddhism could be so damn fun!

ABOUT THE AUTHOR

Photo by Alix Petricek

Jeff Eisenberg was born in Irvington, New Jersey in 1964. He started training in the martial arts as a child and has been training consistently for over 45 years. He is a Grand Master level martial arts instructor, with over 30 years of teaching experience, and ran his own dojo for almost 15 years.

Always priding himself on being a student, he has repeatedly taken off his black belt to put on a white belt and pursue training in a new style. This has taken him on an extensive journey through the martial arts of judo, karate, muay Thai, kali, escrima, hapkido, aikido, and Japanese jiu jitsu. His current martial arts pursuit is Brazilian jiu jitsu, in which he's been training for the last eight years. He is also a certified protection specialist and defensive tactics instructor and has worked as a bodyguard and investigator.

He was first introduced to meditation through his martial arts training, and this introduction began his lifelong interest in mental discipline and Eastern philosophy, particularly Buddhism, which he has been practicing for most of his adult life. In his first book, *Fighting Buddha*, Jeff explores how the two seemingly opposing disciplines he has studied throughout his life can actually support and supplement each other.

Jeff currently lives with his wife, Linda, and a bunch of cats across the street from the beach at the Jersey Shore. For more information and contact visit his website: *fightingbuddhadojo.com*

Also visit the author for exclusive video Dharma talks and instructional martial arts videos at *patreon.com/FightingBuddhaDojo*